IAIN BEASON

Engineering Success

Harness the Power of Staffing, Retain Talent, and Skyrocket Your Revenue

Copyright © 2024 by Iain Beason

All rights reserved. No part of this publication may be reproduced, distributed, or transmitted in any form or by any means, including photocopying, recording, or other electronic or mechanical methods, without the prior written permission of the publisher, except in the case of brief quotations embodied in critical reviews and certain other noncommercial uses permitted by copyright law. This publication is designed to provide accurate and authoritative information in regard to the subject matter covered.

Published by Beason Recruitment Group Ltd..

This book is sold with the understanding that the author and publisher are not engaged in rendering legal, accounting, or other professional services. If professional assistance is required, the services of a competent professional person should be sought. Neither the publisher nor the author shall be liable for damages arising herefrom.

The fact that an organisation or website is referred to in this work as a citation and/or potential source of further information does not mean that the author or the publisher endorses the information the organisation or website may provide or recommendations it may make.

The strategies, advice and techniques described herein are provided for informational purposes only. The author and publisher do not guarantee any specific results and you should consult a professional before making any financial decisions. The publisher and author disclaim any liability, loss, or risk taken by individuals who directly or indirectly act on the information contained herein. All readers are encouraged to seek professional advice when needed.

First edition

*This book was professionally typeset on Reedsy.
Find out more at reedsy.com*

Contents

IMPORTANT READ THIS FIRST	vi
The Vicious Circle of Talent Drain	viii
INTRODUCTION	xi
1 MASTERING THE ART OF HIRING IN MANUFACTURING AND ENGINEERING	1
Understanding Your Recruiting Needs	1
The Art of Writing Job Descriptions	4
Sourcing Candidates: Beyond Job Boards	6
RECAP AND ACTION ITEMS	9
2 THE SECRET SAUCE FOR ATTRACTING TOP TALENT	11
Building an Employer Brand	11
The Role of Company Culture	14
Competitive Compensation and Benefits	17
RECAP AND ACTION ITEMS	20
3 TURNING INTERVIEWS INTO JOB OFFERS	22
Conducting Effective Interviews	22
Selling Your Company to Candidates	25
Making a Competitive Job Offer	27
RECAP AND ACTION ITEMS	30
4 RETAINING STAFF IN A COMPETITIVE MARKET	32
Employee Engagement Strategies	32
Career Development and Progression	35
Maintaining a Healthy Work Environment	38

RECAP AND ACTION ITEMS	41
5 LEVERAGING RECRUITMENT AGENCIES FOR SUCCESS	43
The Role of Recruitment Agencies	43
Choosing the Right Recruitment Agency	45
Working with Your Recruitment Agency	48
RECAP AND ACTION ITEMS	51
6 THE FUTURE OF RECRUITMENT IN MANUFACTURING AND ENGINEERING	53
The Impact of Technology	53
The Role of Data in Recruitment	56
Preparing for Future Skills Needs	59
Summary	61
RECAP AND ACTION ITEMS	62
7 OVERCOMING RECRUITMENT CHALLENGES	65
Dealing with Skills Shortages	65
Reducing Time to Hire	68
Managing Hiring Costs	71
RECAP AND ACTION ITEMS:	74
8 BUILDING A HIGH-PERFORMING TEAM	76
The Importance of Team Dynamics	76
Developing Leadership Skills	79
Creating a Culture of Excellence	82
RECAP AND ACTION ITEMS:	84
9 THE ROLE OF HR IN RECRUITMENT AND RETENTION	87
Building a Strong HR Team	87
HR Policies and Procedures	90
HR's Role in Employee Engagement	93
RECAP AND ACTION ITEMS	96
10 MEASURING RECRUITMENT SUCCESS	98
Key Recruitment Metrics	98

Employee Retention Metrics	101
Using Metrics for Continuous Improvement	103
RECAP AND ACTION ITEMS	106
ENGINEERING YOUR FUTURE SUCCESS, TODAY!	109

IMPORTANT READ THIS FIRST

Hi, I'm Iain Beason, and I'm grateful you chose to delve into this insightful book. I am eager to share my journey and learnings with you, to provide answers to the burning questions you might have about the recruitment agency industry. With over 15 years of experience in the recruitment and consultancy industries, I have identified and debunked numerous misconceptions. This book is my effort to enlighten you and guide your path towards successful staffing solutions.

After all, maybe you've experienced the frustration of sourcing top candidates for your manufacturing business. The struggle of finding those individuals with the right skills, qualifications, and experience that align with your company's vision and goals can be a daunting task. And retaining them? That's an entirely different challenge.

Maybe you've grappled with the vicious cycle of high employee turnover in your business. The constant need to refill positions, the time and resources spent on training, only to have these individuals leave for greener pastures. The drain on your company's morale and productivity can be disheartening.

Or maybe you've even faced the conundrum of stagnant sales and revenue, a direct consequence of not being able to attract and retain top talent. The correlation might not be evident initially, but it's a harsh reality for many businesses.

And look, I get it, it's not fair.

The truth is, you're not alone. It seems most manufacturing and engineering businesses are victims of this staffing dilemma. The struggle to attract top candidates, retain them, and ultimately boost sales and revenue is a widespread issue.

That feeling of helplessness, frustration, and anxiety you're experiencing is shared by many in your shoes. It's an overwhelming sense of being stuck in a vicious cycle, unable to break free and propel your business forward.

Here's what most don't realise: The root of these issues often lies deeper than just recruitment strategies. It involves the whole ecosystem of your business, from your company culture to compensation models, and even your leadership style.

And now with the possibility of a widening skills gap in the industry, the challenges of attracting top candidates and retaining them are only set to increase. The stakes are high, and the margin for error is shrinking.

It seems most are left in a state of uncertainty and fear. The fear of being unable to sustain your business, of falling behind in the competition, and of not realising your company's true potential due to staffing issues. But remember, understanding the problem is the first step towards finding a solution.

The Vicious Circle of Talent Drain

In the world of manufacturing and precision engineering, there is a cycle, a perpetual loop of frustration and disappointment, that many business owners find themselves trapped within. This loop, known as the Vicious Circle of Talent Drain, is a ceaseless cycle that hinders the growth of businesses and stunts the rise in revenue. In the following paragraphs, we'll delve into the intricate workings of this cycle, detailing each painstaking step and the reasons why it perpetually repeats itself.

Endless Search

Perhaps you've found yourself in an endless search, pouring over resumes, interviewing potential candidates, but to no avail. The right person for the job seems to be just out of reach, an elusive figure hidden within the masses. This continuous hunt for talent is not only time-consuming but incredibly disheartening. It feels like trying to find a needle in a haystack, and this frustration eventually leads to the next step in the cycle, the Compromise.

Compromise

In your desperation to fill the vacant position, you're forced to compromise, to settle for someone who is not quite right but will do for now. This compromise feels like an uneasy truce, a decision made out of necessity rather than choice. But the decision to compromise not only affects the quality of work but also the morale of your existing team. This dissatisfaction leads you to the next stage, the Exodus.

Exodus

The compromise not only affects your business's performance but also the morale of your existing team. This decline in morale leads to an exodus, where your top performers start looking out for better opportunities. You find yourself losing your star players, the very backbone of your business, pushing you towards the next phase, the Panic.

Panic

The loss of your top performers sends you into a state of panic, a frenzied attempt to fill the void left behind by their exit. You scramble, trying to find replacements, but the pressure and urgency often lead to poor hiring decisions. And thus, you find yourself back at the first stage, the Endless Search.

Repetition

You find yourself back at square one, starting the process all over again. The repetitive nature of the circle gives off a false sense of progress, a deceptive feeling of movement. But in reality, you're stuck in the same place, caught in the relentless loop of the Vicious Circle of Talent Drain.

The cycle clearly indicates that a different approach is needed to attract top candidates, retain them in your business, and thereby enhance your sales and revenue. This continuous loop of frustration and disappointment only leads to stagnation. It's imperative to break free from this cycle if you wish to see real growth and progress in your business.

I'm thrilled that you're reading this book. As you delve deeper into the subsequent chapters, you will discover the solutions you've been seeking. The insight you gain from this book will empower you to break free from the Vicious Circle of Talent Drain and elevate your business to new heights.

INTRODUCTION

Imagine for a moment, you are at the helm of a world-class engineering or manufacturing company. Picture a team of dedicated, talented and driven individuals, all working together to create products and services that are not just good, but extraordinary. These people are not just employees; they are the lifeblood of your company, the heart and soul of your success. Sounds like a dream, right? Well, it doesn't have to be. This is the reality we are going to help you create.

The landscape of the engineering and manufacturing industry is rapidly changing. With the rise of automation, artificial intelligence, and evolving customer demands, the need for top-notch talent has never been more critical. The challenge of finding, attracting, and retaining this talent, however, is a hurdle that many businesses face.

The first part of our journey together will focus on mastering the art of hiring in the manufacturing and engineering arena. We'll delve into the secret sauce for attracting top talent, turning interviews into job offers, and retaining staff in today's competitive market. We will guide you to cultivate a company culture that not only attracts the crème de la crème but also makes them want to stay for the long haul.

In the second part, we will explore how to leverage recruitment agencies for success. Agencies can be a powerful ally in your quest for talent, providing you with a pool of qualified candidates and freeing up your time to focus on what you do best: running your business. Additionally, we will take a peek into the future of recruitment in our industry, exploring emerging trends and how you can adapt to stay ahead of the curve.

Finally, in the third part, we will tackle the challenges of recruitment head-on. We will share strategies and insights for overcoming these obstacles, building a high-performing team, and the crucial role of HR in recruitment and retention. We will also delve into how to measure recruitment success, equipping you with the tools to continually evaluate and improve your hiring process.

Throughout this book, you will find the practical, actionable advice you need to navigate the often choppy waters of recruitment and retention. This isn't just theory; these are tried and tested strategies that have been proven to work in the real world.

The goal is simple: to help you build a team that is as passionate about your business as you are. A team that is expertly skilled, consistently motivated, and fiercely loyal. A team that doesn't just meet your expectations but exceeds them, propelling your business to heights of success you have only dreamed of.

Remember, this isn't just about hiring. It's about creating a powerful, sustainable competitive advantage for your business. It's about turning your company into a talent magnet, a place where the best and brightest want to work. It's about building a team that can withstand the challenges of the rapidly evolving engineering and manufacturing industry and come out on top.

So, are you ready to take this journey with us? Are you ready to harness the power of staffing, retain top talent, and skyrocket your revenue? Are you ready to turn your business into a powerhouse of productivity, innovation, and success? Then let's get started. The future of your business depends on it.

After all, as the saying goes, "you're only as good as the team you have behind you." Now, let's get to work on building yours.

1

MASTERING THE ART OF HIRING IN MANUFACTURING AND ENGINEERING

"Success usually comes to those who are too busy to be looking for it." - Henry David Thoreau

Understanding Your Recruiting Needs

How are you going to find the right people to drive your business forward if you don't know who or what you're looking for? It's like trying to hit a dartboard blindfolded - not exactly the recipe for success. Let's go through how you can understand your recruiting needs better.

Recognising Skills Gaps

First things first, understanding what you need starts with a clear view of what you currently have. It's time to assess your team's skills. Start by listing down the essential skills required to keep the cogs of your manufacturing or engineering firm turning. Now, match these skills against your current team. Do they all add up? If not, you've found your skills gaps.

This exercise isn't designed to make you feel inadequate; it's about identifying areas for improvement. You wouldn't expect a welder to operate a CNC machine without training, would you? Similarly, you shouldn't expect your business to perform well if your team lacks the necessary skills.

Remember, skills gaps aren't just about hard skills. Soft skills like leadership, communication, and team collaboration can be just as critical in a manufacturing or engineering environment.

Defining Job Requirements

Now that you have your skills gaps identified, it's time to turn them into job requirements. This is where you need to get specific. For example, if you've identified a need for CNC programming skills, your job requirement might be: "Experience in CNC programming and ability to read and interpret engineering drawings."

The more specific you can be, the better. Aim to list down about 5-7 key job requirements. Why this number? It's a sweet spot. Too few, and you risk attracting unqualified candidates. Too many, and you might scare off potential talent.

Don't forget to consider the level of expertise required. Do you need a seasoned expert or can you afford to train a promising novice? Remember, hiring isn't just about filling a position; it's about investing in your company's future.

Setting Candidate Expectations

This is where many hiring managers drop the ball. Remember, it's not just about what the candidate can do for you, but also what you can do for them.

Candidates today are savvy; they want to know what's in it for them. So, make sure you're clear about what they can expect from joining your team. This could be anything from the opportunity to work with cutting-edge technology, to the chance to lead a team or contribute to exciting projects.

At the same time, be upfront about the challenges they might face. Is it a high-pressure role with tight deadlines? Will they need to work independently most of the time? Being transparent from the get-go can prevent misunderstandings later on.

In conclusion, understanding your recruiting needs is about more than just knowing what skills you're short of. It's about understanding what you can offer as an employer and setting clear expectations from the start. This way, you'll attract candidates who are not only capable but also motivated and ready to contribute to your team's success.

So, take some time to sit down and truly understand your recruiting needs. It's the first step towards engineering your success. Remember, it's not just about filling a vacancy; it's about finding the right person who can help your business grow. After all, your team is your biggest asset.

The Art of Writing Job Descriptions

Unveiling the art of writing job descriptions is like decoding the DNA of your company. It's about more than just listing the skills needed for a role; it's about capturing the essence of your company culture, the growth opportunities you offer, and the unique benefits that set you apart from other employers in the manufacturing and engineering industries.

Crafting Compelling Job Posts

Writing a job description is a bit like writing a love letter to your ideal candidate. You're trying to woo them, to convince them that your company is the perfect match for their skills and aspirations. The key here is to be authentic and genuine. Start with the position title and then move on to a brief overview of the role. This should be a concise snapshot of what the job involves, leaving the reader with a clear picture of what a typical day in the role might look like.

Next, outline the responsibilities of the position. Be specific and use active verbs. Instead of saying, "Assistance may be required in..." say, "You will be responsible for...". This kind of language paints a more vivid picture and helps potential candidates to visualise themselves in the role.

But remember, this isn't a shopping list. Don't overwhelm candidates with a laundry list of duties - focus on the most critical and unique aspects of the job.

Highlighting Company Culture

Your company culture is what sets you apart from other employers. It's the invisible glue that holds your team together and it's a crucial factor for many job seekers. So, how can you showcase your culture in a job description?

Start by describing the work environment. Is it fast-paced and dynamic, or more laid back and flexible? Do you have a flat hierarchy where everyone's ideas are valued, or do you adhere to more traditional organisational structures?

Next, talk about your values. What beliefs and principles guide your decisions and actions? Perhaps you prioritise innovation and creativity, or maybe you value teamwork and collaboration above all else. Whatever your core values are, make sure they shine through in your job description.

Finally, talk about the perks. Do you offer flexible working hours, generous holiday allowances, or unique training opportunities? These can be real deal-breakers for potential candidates and can help you to attract top talent.

Emphasising Growth Opportunities

For many candidates, particularly in the manufacturing and engineering industries, the chance to grow and develop is a key consideration when choosing an employer. So, make sure your job description paints a clear picture of the growth opportunities on offer.

Rather than burying this information in the 'benefits' section, weave it throughout your job description. On top of mentioning it in the general overview, you might discuss specific growth opportunities when outlining the job's responsibilities. For example, you could say, "You'll work closely with our senior engineers, gaining invaluable experience and learning from the best in the industry."

Remember, growth isn't just about promotions and pay rises. It also means developing new skills, expanding your knowledge base, and tackling new and exciting challenges. It's about becoming a better version of yourself, both personally and professionally. Make sure this message radiates from every line of your job description.

So there you have it. The art of writing job descriptions is all about authenticity, precision, and a dash of creativity. It's about telling a compelling story that captures the essence of your company and the role in question, while also painting an enticing picture of the future. It's not always easy, but when done right, it can transform your recruitment process and help you to attract and retain the top talent in the manufacturing and engineering industries.

Sourcing Candidates: Beyond Job Boards

In the world of manufacturing and engineering, you know the importance of having the right people on your team. Engineers, welders, CNC operators – these are not roles you can fill with just anyone. It's not enough to post a job ad and hope for the best. You need to actively source the right candidates. So, where do you start? Let's explore three avenues beyond job boards - recruitment agencies, social media, and employee referrals.

Leveraging Recruitment Agencies

Recruitment agencies can be a real game-changer when it comes to sourcing candidates. These industry insiders often have a wide network of contacts and understand the specifics of the roles you're looking to fill. They can save you a lot of time and effort by weeding out unqualified candidates and presenting you with a shortlist of potential hires.

However, not all agencies are created equal. It's important that you choose one with a deep understanding of the manufacturing and engineering industry. Look for agencies that specialise in your industry and have a track record of successful placements. Ask for case studies or testimonials if they're not readily available.

Remember, a good recruitment agency should feel like an extension of your HR team. They should take the time to understand your business, your culture, and the specific needs of the role. If they're not asking the right questions or seem more interested in filling the role quickly than finding the right fit, it might be time to look elsewhere.

Using Social Media for Recruitment

Social media is not just for sharing holiday snaps and funny cat videos. It's also a powerful tool for recruitment. Sites like LinkedIn, Facebook, and even Instagram can be a treasure trove of potential candidates.

LinkedIn is undoubtedly the go-to platform for professional networking. You can use it to advertise vacancies, but also to actively headhunt. Look for people with the right skills and experience and don't be afraid to reach out to them directly. Remember, even if they're not actively looking for a new role, they might be open to a conversation.

Facebook and Instagram might seem less obvious choices, but they can be effective, especially if you're looking to reach a younger demographic. Use these platforms to showcase your company culture and highlight the opportunities for growth and development within your company.

Remember, it's not enough to just post a job ad and hope for the best. Engage with your audience, respond to comments and messages, and show that you're a company people would want to work for.

Relying on Employee Referrals

Lastly, but by no means least, don't underestimate the power of employee referrals. Your current team members can be your best recruiters. They understand your company culture, they know the ins and outs of the job, and they likely have a network of contacts in the industry.

Consider implementing an employee referral scheme. Incentivising your team to refer candidates can significantly increase the number of quality applicants. The incentives don't have to be huge — a bonus, an extra day off, or even a small gift can be enough to motivate your team.

But remember, a successful referral scheme relies on having a happy and engaged workforce. If your team members enjoy their jobs and feel valued, they'll be more likely to recommend your company to their friends and contacts.

So there you have it, three strategies for sourcing candidates beyond job boards. Leveraging recruitment agencies, using social media for recruitment, and relying on employee referrals can all be effective ways to find the right people for your team. The key is to be proactive and think outside the box. After all, in the world of manufacturing and engineering, it's your team that will make or break your success.

RECAP AND ACTION ITEMS

We've traversed the rugged terrain of hiring in the manufacturing and engineering sectors, dissecting the importance of understanding your recruiting needs, the art of crafting compelling job descriptions, and the savvy of sourcing candidates beyond just job boards.

Now, it's time to implement. Here's your action plan, no fluff, just straightforward strategies.

First, audit your teams. Recognise the skills gaps and define the precise job requirements needed to fill these voids. Be as specific as you can. List out the must-have skills and those that would be nice to have. This will give you a clear picture of your ideal candidate.

Next, write a job description that sells. Remember, this is your chance to sell your company to prospective candidates. Highlight your unique company culture and the growth opportunities that await the right candidate. Don't just list out the job responsibilities. Make it appealing and real.

Now, let's shake up the sourcing game. Look beyond the traditional job boards. Leverage recruitment agencies with a proven track record in your industry. Tap into the vast reservoir of talent on social media. And don't forget about employee referrals - your existing team could be sitting on a goldmine of potential hires.

Finally, remember that hiring isn't a one-and-done deal. It's an ongoing process of refining and improving your methods to attract, hire, and retain top talent.

Take these action steps and you'll transform your hiring process, ensuring you attract the right talent to drive your business forward. Master these steps, and you're not just hiring—you're building a powerhouse team that fuels the engine of your company's success.

Remember, in the world of engineering and manufacturing, the quality of your staff is as important as the quality of your machinery. So, invest in your hiring process like you would invest in a new CNC machine. The returns will be worth it.

Now, go out there and engineer your success. You've got this

2

THE SECRET SAUCE FOR ATTRACTING TOP TALENT

"Success is not the key to happiness. Happiness is the key to success. If you love what you are doing, you will be successful." – Albert Schweitzer

Building an Employer Brand

As you navigate the challenging seas of business ownership, your compass should always point towards the magnetic north of attracting top talent. One of the most effective ways to do this is by building a robust employer brand. Think of it as the reputation your company has in the minds of potential employees. It's what they think when they hear your company's name. It's their perception of what it'd be like to work for you. And it's absolutely crucial if you want to attract the best of the best.

Enhancing Company Reputation

Many business owners make the mistake of thinking their company's reputation is entirely based on the quality of their products or services. That's only part of the story. Your reputation as an employer is equally, if not more, important. The good news is, there are concrete steps you can take to enhance your reputation and make your company a magnet for top talent.

First off, be sure to promote the accomplishments of your team. Whether it's a welder who's become a master of their craft, or a CNC machinist who's constantly innovating, make it a point to sing their praises. Not only does this boost morale, but it also shows potential employees that your company recognises and values hard work and skill.

Next, don't be shy about publicising any awards or recognition your company has earned. Whether it's an industry award for innovation or a local business award for community service, these accolades help to build your reputation as a top-tier employer.

Finally, remember that transparency is key. In an age where information is just a Google search away, potential employees will be able to see if your company's actions match its words. So, don't just talk about being a great place to work. Show it through your actions.

Emphasising Employee Benefits

A big part of what makes a company attractive to potential employees is the benefits it offers. And no, I'm not just talking about free coffee or a snazzy office. I'm talking about benefits that truly make a difference in the lives of your employees.

For instance, perhaps you could offer flexible working hours. This is especially attractive to employees with families, as it allows them to better balance their work and home lives. Or perhaps you could offer additional training and development opportunities. This shows potential employees that you're invested in their growth and advancement.

Oh, and don't forget to emphasise the unique benefits that come with working in the manufacturing and engineering industries. Whether it's the satisfaction of creating tangible products, the opportunity to work with cutting-edge technology, or the chance to be a part of a close-knit team, these are all things that can make your company stand out.

Showcasing Company Values

Finally, let's talk about company values. These days, it's not enough to just offer a competitive salary and a decent benefits package. More and more, employees are looking for companies whose values align with their own.

So, what are your company's values? Maybe you're committed to sustainability and green manufacturing practices. Or maybe you believe in the importance of continuous learning and innovation. Whatever your values are, make sure they're front and centre in your employer branding efforts.

Not only will this help to attract like-minded individuals, but it will also help to create a sense of unity and purpose within your team. After all, when everyone is pulling in the same direction, that's when truly great things happen.

So, there you have it. Building a strong employer brand isn't rocket science, but it does require thought, effort, and a genuine commitment to creating a workplace that people love. By enhancing your company's reputation, emphasising the right benefits, and showcasing your values, you'll be well on your way to becoming a top choice for the best talent in the industry. And that, my friend, is a recipe for success.

The Role of Company Culture

One of the key elements in attracting top talent and retaining them in your organisation is the company culture. It's like the secret sauce that can make or break your employee experience. So let's dive into what this company culture thing is all about and how you can use it to your advantage.

Creating a Positive Work Environment

Let's start with the physical workplace. Look around your shop floor, your office, or your workstation. What does it say about your company? Is it a clean, safe, and welcoming place? Or does it scream 'just another drab workspace'?

You see, a positive work environment goes beyond just having a clean and safe place. It means creating an atmosphere where employees feel valued, heard, and respected. It's about ensuring that your team feels comfortable coming forward with new ideas or concerns.

Think about the little things that can make a big difference in your employees' day-to-day lives. It could be as simple as providing comfortable chairs or a break room with a coffee machine. Maybe it's a quiet room where employees can relax or meditate. You could even introduce flexi-time or remote working options to help your team achieve a better work-life balance.

Remember, a positive work environment isn't just about the physical space. It's about the emotional and psychological space you create for your staff. It's about respect, appreciation, and making each person feel like they belong.

Encouraging Team Collaboration

Now, let's talk team collaboration. This is where the magic happens. When your team works together well, they can achieve more than they ever could alone. They can solve problems faster, innovate more effectively, and deliver better results for your business.

But collaboration isn't something that just happens. It's something you need to actively foster and promote. One way to do this is by setting up cross-functional teams. This encourages people from different departments or areas of expertise to work together on projects. It can lead to fresh ideas, new perspectives, and innovative solutions to problems.

Encourage open communication and provide platforms that make it easy for your team to collaborate. This could be online tools like Slack or Microsoft Teams, or physical spaces like meeting rooms or brainstorming areas.

Also, remember that collaboration should be a two-way street. Encourage your team to share their ideas and give feedback. This will make them feel valued and help foster a culture of continuous improvement.

Promoting Work-Life Balance

Finally, let's talk about work-life balance. This is a big one. Many top talents are looking for more than just a paycheck. They want a job that allows them to have a life outside of work. They want to be able to spend time with their families, pursue hobbies, or just relax and recharge.

So, how can you promote work-life balance in your company? Start by respecting your employees' time. Avoid expecting them to work long hours or be available 24/7. Encourage them to take breaks and use their holiday time.

You could also introduce flexible working arrangements. This could be allowing your employees to work from home a few days a week, or offering flexible start and finish times. This can help your team to manage their work around their personal commitments.

One more thing to consider is offering wellness programs. This could be anything from discounted gym memberships to meditation classes or mental health support. It shows that you care about your employees' wellbeing and can help to reduce stress and burnout.

In short, promoting a work-life balance is about understanding that your employees are human beings with lives outside of work. It's about respecting their time, their needs, and their wellbeing.

So, there you have it. The role of company culture in attracting top talent. It's about creating a positive work environment, encouraging team collaboration, and promoting work-life balance. By focusing on these areas, you can create a company culture that attracts top talent and keeps them around for the long run. And that, my friends, can be the secret sauce to skyrocketing your revenue.

Competitive Compensation and Benefits

Benchmarking Salaries

In the world of engineering and manufacturing, it's no secret that a competitive salary can make or break a deal for top talent. It's about acknowledging the value of their skills, their experience, and their potential contribution to your company. But how do you determine what's competitive? The answer lies in benchmarking.

Benchmarking salaries is not a one-off activity. It's a continuous process of comparing your company's salary scales with those of similar companies in the industry. This will give you an insight into what your competitors are offering and help you to stay ahead in the race. It's like keeping your finger on the pulse of the industry, staying in tune with the rhythm of the market rates.

To do this, you can use tools like industry surveys, online resources, and external consultancies. You might also want to consider geographical variations in the cost of living, the size and turnover of your company, and the current economic climate. Keep in mind that you're not just trying to match the competition – you're aiming to outdo them.

But remember, it's not just about the money. As Tim Ferris puts it, 'Money is multiplied in practical value depending on the number of W's you control in your life: what you do, when you do it, where you do it, and with whom you do it.' A competitive salary is just the base; the real value lies in how much control and flexibility your employees have in their work-life.

Offering Unique Perks

Now let's talk about perks. Not just any perks, but unique perks. These are the extras that can give you the edge when attracting top talent. They're what make your company stand out from the crowd.

You could consider offering flexible working hours or the option to work remotely. With technology making it easier than ever to work from anywhere, these perks are becoming increasingly valuable to employees.

You might also want to think about professional development opportunities. This could be anything from training courses and mentoring programs to attending industry conferences and events. Remember, in the engineering and manufacturing industries, staying on top of the latest technologies and trends is crucial. It's not just about personal growth, but also about staying competitive in a rapidly evolving industry.

Another unique perk could be offering shares in the company. This not only serves as a financial incentive but also gives employees a sense of ownership and involvement in the company's success. After all, who wouldn't want to feel like they're part of something bigger than themselves?

Investing in Employee Health and Wellness

Finally, let's talk about health and wellness. It's an area that's often overlooked, but it plays a crucial role in attracting and retaining top talent.

Investing in your employees' health and wellness isn't just about offering a gym membership (though that's a good start). It's about creating a work environment that promotes physical and mental well-being. This could mean offering healthy snacks in the office, organising team sports activities, or even providing onsite health check-ups.

Mental health is equally important. Consider offering support for stress management, such as counselling services or mindfulness workshops. Encourage a culture where it's okay to take a break when needed and ensure that workloads are manageable.

Remember, a happy, healthy employee is a productive, motivated employee – and that's a win-win for both you and your team.

So there you have it. Competitive compensation and benefits are about much more than just money. It's about acknowledging the value of your employees, offering unique perks that set you apart from the competition, and investing in the health and wellness of your team. It's about creating an environment where top talent doesn't just want to work, but wants to stay and grow with your company. That's the secret sauce for attracting top talent in the engineering and manufacturing industries.

RECAP AND ACTION ITEMS

You've made it through the meat and potatoes of The Secret Sauce for Attracting Top Talent. Let's quickly recap what we've unpacked.

In building an employer brand, remember it's all about enhancing your reputation, emphasising benefits for employees, and showcasing your company values. This isn't just about attracting talent, it's about retaining it. If your company is a place people want to work, they'll stick around.

Company culture is equally important. A positive work environment, team collaboration, and a proper work-life balance all play into this. Make your company a place where people feel valued and they'll be more likely to perform at their best.

And finally, competitive compensation and benefits. It's not just about the money, although that's important too. Offering unique perks and investing in employee health and wellness can make your company stand out from the crowd.

So, what are your action items?

First, carry out an audit of your company's reputation. Identify any negative perceptions and address them head-on. Promote your company's benefits and values in recruitment materials and on your website.

Next, assess your company culture. Encourage feedback from employees and implement changes where necessary. Foster a positive work environment and encourage team collaboration. And remember, a healthy work-life balance isn't a luxury, it's a necessity.

Finally, benchmark your salaries against the industry standard and offer competitive compensation. And don't forget the perks! From gym memberships to extra holiday days, these can make all the difference. Plus, invest in employee health and wellness. A healthy team is a productive team.

Now, it's time to turn these insights into action. Attracting top talent isn't an overnight process, but with the right strategies in place, you can transform your company into a talent magnet. So, go forth, implement, and watch your business skyrocket.

3

TURNING INTERVIEWS INTO JOB OFFERS

"Hire character. Train skill." – Peter Schutz

Conducting Effective Interviews

Kickstarting this journey, let's dive into the art of conducting effective interviews. Interviews are your golden ticket to finding the best talent in the market. But how can you ensure you're getting the most out of them? It's all about asking the right questions, assessing candidate fit and making candidates feel comfortable.

Asking the Right Questions

The power of an interview lies in the questions you ask. Don't just throw out generic questions and expect to find a diamond in the rough. You need to tailor your questions to the role, the industry and your company's culture.

Start with technical questions that are related to the job role. For instance, if you're interviewing for a welding position, you could ask questions like, "Can you describe your experience with welding materials such as aluminium or stainless steel?" or "Can you explain how you would go about joining two pieces of metal together?" These questions will help you gauge their practical knowledge and experience in the field.

Next, delve into behavioural questions to understand how they handle certain situations. A good question might be, "Tell me about a time when you faced a significant challenge on a project. How did you handle it?" Their answer can give you insight into their problem-solving abilities, resilience, and how they function under pressure.

Finally, don't forget to ask about their career goals. This might seem to be a soft question, but it's crucial. If your candidate's ambitions align with your company's path, you've probably got a keeper.

Assessing Candidate Fit

Now, let's talk about assessing candidate fit. Remember, you're not just looking for someone who can do the job; you're looking for someone who can thrive in your company culture. You want someone who shares your company's values, fits in with the team and is motivated by the same things that drive your company forward.

There are a few ways you can assess this. First, watch how they interact with you and others during the interview. Are they respectful, friendly, and engaged? These are good signs they'll fit in with your team.

Second, listen carefully to their answers. Do they talk about teamwork, innovation, quality – whatever it is that your company values? If yes, they're probably a good cultural fit.

Lastly, consider their long-term goals. If they're looking for a stepping stone to another industry or role, they might not be the best fit for your company.

Making Candidates Feel Comfortable

The last piece of the puzzle is making candidates feel comfortable. Interviews can be nerve-wracking, and when candidates are nervous, they may not perform at their best. It's your job to create an environment where they can truly shine.

Start by setting clear expectations for the interview. Let them know the format, who they'll be speaking with, and what kinds of questions they can expect. This can help to alleviate any pre-interview jitters.

During the interview, be mindful of your body language. Maintain eye contact, nod to show you're listening and keep your posture open. This shows the candidate that you're engaged and interested in what they have to say.

Finally, make sure to give them time to ask their own questions. This isn't just about you assessing them – they're assessing you too. By allowing them to ask questions, you're showing that you value their input and are interested in what they have to say.

Conducting effective interviews isn't rocket science, but it does require some thought and preparation. By asking the right questions, assessing candidate fit, and making candidates feel comfortable, you're well on your way to finding the perfect candidate for your engineering or manufacturing business.

Selling Your Company to Candidates

Let's dive right in. The first step is all about highlighting your company's strengths.

Highlighting Company Strengths

In the world of engineering and manufacturing, you're not just selling a job; you're selling a career, a lifestyle, and perhaps most importantly, a mission. Your company's strengths are the backbone of this selling point. This isn't just about financial stability or market position, although those are important. It's about the problems you solve, the innovations you drive, and the value you create.

Part of this process is understanding what engineers value. They want to know that their work has a purpose, that they'll have opportunities to learn and grow, and that they'll be working with cutting-edge technology. These are your selling points. Whether you're developing new welding techniques, pioneering CNC applications, or pushing the boundaries of what's possible in manufacturing, these are the stories you need to tell.

But remember, candidates are not just interested in what you do, but how you do it. A positive company culture, a commitment to work-life balance, and a supportive environment can be just as attractive as a high-profile project. So don't forget to highlight these aspects during the interview process.

Discussing Future Opportunities

The next step is to discuss future opportunities. Engineers are innovators by nature. They're always looking forward, always eager to tackle the next challenge. This is why it's so crucial to show them not just where your company is now, but where it's going in the future.

Talk about your vision for the future. What are your goals? What are the challenges you anticipate? How do you plan to grow and evolve? This not only gives candidates a sense of direction, but also shows them where they fit into the bigger picture.

Don't shy away from discussing specific roles or projects they might be involved in. Show them how they can contribute and make a difference. Be clear about the career progression and learning opportunities. Remember, you're selling a journey, not just a job.

Addressing Candidate Concerns

Finally, it's about addressing candidate concerns. This is your chance to reassure candidates that your company is a great place to work. This could involve discussing your company's response to issues like job security, work-life balance, and employee wellness.

For example, in the engineering industry, mental health and stress are significant concerns. If your company has a strong support system in place, such as flexible working hours or mental health resources, make sure to mention these during the interview.

Likewise, if a candidate is concerned about job security, talk about your company's stability, your position in the market, and your plans for future growth. If they're worried about career progression, discuss the opportunities for advancement within your company and the resources available for professional development.

Making a Competitive Job Offer

When it comes to securing top talent in the engineering and manufacturing industry, making a competitive job offer is where the rubber meets the road. It's not just about throwing numbers at a candidate but crafting an offer that is appealing, justifiable, and competitive. This includes the art of negotiating salaries, offering unique perks, and the finesse of closing the deal.

Negotiating Salaries

Let's kick off with negotiating salaries. As a business owner, you likely already understand the need to balance the books and keep costs under control. However, when it comes to attracting top talent in industries like welding and CNC, it's crucial to offer a salary package that reflects the market rate and the value the candidate brings to your company.

Firstly, do your research. Investigate the current market rate for the role you're hiring for, taking into account the candidate's experience level and the region in which your company operates. Websites such as Glassdoor and Payscale can provide useful insights, as can speaking to industry peers or recruiting professionals.

When it comes to the actual negotiation, remember that transparency and honesty are key. If your offer is below the candidate's expectations, explain your reasoning. Perhaps there are other elements of the compensation package that make up for a lower base salary. Or maybe there are opportunities for rapid advancement and salary growth within your company.

Offering Unique Perks

In today's competitive job market, salary alone may not cut the mustard. That's where perks come in. Perks not only sweeten the deal, they also help differentiate your company from the competition. They show that you value your employees and are invested in their happiness and wellbeing.

Perks can range from flexible working hours and remote work options, which are increasingly important in today's digital, post-pandemic world, to more industry-specific benefits. For example, in the welding and CNC industries, perks could include ongoing training and certification opportunities, state-of-the-art equipment, or even allowances for personal protective equipment (PPE) and workwear.

Remember, the best perks are those that align with your company culture and values, as well as the desires and needs of your employees. So, don't be afraid to think outside the box and offer perks that are unique to your company.

Closing the Deal

Finally, let's talk about closing the deal. This is arguably the most important part of the process, as it's where you seal the commitment from your candidate.

Start by reiterating the value proposition of the job offer. Highlight the salary, perks, and opportunities for growth within your company. But also remind them of the non-tangible benefits, such as the chance to work on exciting projects, be part of an innovative team, or make a difference in the industry.

Once you've laid out the offer, give the candidate time to consider it. Don't rush them into making a decision. Remember, accepting a job is a significant decision and they'll appreciate having the time to mull it over.

When they're ready to respond, be prepared to handle objections or counter-offers. If they ask for a higher salary or additional perks, don't dismiss them outright. Instead, take the time to consider their request. If you can't meet it, explain why and try to offer an alternative solution.

Making a competitive job offer is as much an art as it is a

science. By mastering the skills of salary negotiation, offering unique perks, and closing the deal, you'll be well on your way to attracting and retaining the top talent your manufacturing or engineering business needs to skyrocket your revenue. Remember, it's not just about the money, but about creating a package that truly appeals to your candidate and shows them they'd be valued and appreciated in your company.

RECAP AND ACTION ITEMS

So, you've got the inside track on conducting effective interviews, selling your company to candidates, and making a competitive job offer. Let's put it all together and set you on the road to transforming your hiring process.

First, recall the importance of conducting interviews that not only assess a candidate's skills but also fit within your company culture. Remember to ask the right questions, ones that truly probe a candidate's abilities and compatibility. Make your candidates feel comfortable, it's vital for them to show their true colours.

Next, you've got to sell your company to candidates. Highlight your strengths, make sure candidates understand the unique opportunities they'll have access to in your organisation. Address any concerns they may have upfront and openly. Transparency is key.

Finally, when it comes to making a job offer, don't shy away from negotiating salaries. Remember, competitive pay is a surefire way to attract top talent. But it's not all about money.

Offer unique perks that reflect your company's values and culture. And when you're ready to close the deal, do it with confidence and conviction.

Now, for the action items. Start by revising your current interview process. Implement the strategies you've learned about asking the right questions and making candidates feel comfortable. Next, create a clear, compelling narrative about your company to share with potential hires. Highlight your strengths and address potential concerns. Finally, reconsider your job offer strategy. Ensure you're offering competitive salaries and unique perks.

Remember, the hiring process doesn't end when a candidate accepts a job offer. It's just the beginning of a relationship that can significantly impact your business's future. So, implement these strategies, transform your hiring process, and watch how it leads to a surge in your company's success.

This isn't rocket science. It's simply about harnessing the power within your organisation to attract, retain, and nurture top talent. So, what are you waiting for? It's time to turn those interviews into job offers.

4

RETAINING STAFF IN A COMPETITIVE MARKET

"Train people well enough so they can leave, treat them well enough so they don't want to." - Richard Branson

Employee Engagement Strategies

Let's dive right into the first area you need to focus on to retain your staff in a competitive market – employee engagement strategies. Now, this isn't just about putting on a good Christmas party or having a free coffee machine in the breakroom. Employee engagement is a more substantial strategy that involves creating an environment where your employees feel valued, heard, and motivated to contribute to your business's success.

Regular Feedback and Recognition

First things first, let's talk about feedback and recognition. In the whirlwind of running a manufacturing or engineering business, it's easy to forget about the simple act of acknowledging your team's hard work. But remember, a simple 'thank you' or 'well done' can go a long way in making your employees feel valued.

Feedback, both positive and constructive, is crucial for growth. It gives your team a clear understanding of their performance, highlighting their strengths and areas they need to improve. Regular feedback sessions, whether formal or informal, make your employees feel involved and valued. It tells them that their work matters and their efforts are recognised.

Now, let's debunk a misconception. Regular feedback doesn't mean yearly performance reviews. In today's fast-paced world, a year is a long time. If you want to keep your employees engaged, consider introducing monthly or even weekly feedback sessions. This will keep everyone on their toes and continuously striving for improvement.

Recognition, on the other hand, is about celebrating success. This could be anything from a shout-out in a team meeting for a job well done, to more formal methods like 'employee of the month' awards or bonus schemes. Remember, recognition isn't always about financial rewards. Often, a public acknowledgment of good work is just as motivating.

Providing Learning Opportunities

Next up, learning opportunities. The engineering and manufacturing sector is constantly evolving. New technologies, techniques, and methodologies are continually emerging. As such, your employees need to continuously update their skills to stay ahead of the curve.

Providing your team with regular learning opportunities not only helps them improve professionally but also shows that you are invested in their growth. This could be in the form of in-house training sessions, online courses, or even sponsoring them to attend industry conferences and workshops.

Remember, learning is not a one-size-fits-all strategy. Some of your employees may prefer hands-on training, while others may thrive in a more academic setting. It's important to consider individual learning styles and preferences when planning these opportunities.

Encouraging Employee Input

Finally, let's talk about encouraging employee input. This is all about fostering a culture where your team feels comfortable sharing their ideas and opinions.

In engineering and manufacturing businesses, your staff are the ones on the ground, dealing with the nitty-gritty every day. They know the ins and outs of your operations and are likely to have valuable insights that could help improve processes, increase efficiency, or even bring in new business.

By encouraging employee input, you're not only potentially gaining valuable ideas but also making your employees feel heard and valued. This could be as simple as introducing a suggestion box or as involved as holding regular brainstorming sessions or workshops.

Keeping your employees engaged is a vital part of retaining staff in a competitive market. By providing regular feedback and recognition, offering learning opportunities, and encouraging employee input, you're creating an environment where your employees feel motivated and invested in your business's success.

And remember, engagement strategies aren't a one-off task. They need to be continuously reviewed and updated to ensure they're still effective and aligned with your business's goals and your employees' needs.

So, take a moment to reflect on your current strategies. Are they robust enough? Do they make your employees feel valued and heard? If not, it's time to make some changes. After all, a business is only as strong as its team.

Career Development and Progression

In the ever-evolving world of manufacturing and engineering, the phrase "standing still is going backwards" rings true. Your staff's professional growth is vital to your company's success and longevity. Here, we delve into career development and progression strategies that can help you keep your talented workforce engaged, motivated, and committed.

Offering Training and Development

At the heart of any successful manufacturing or CNC business lies a team that is constantly upskilling. The question is, how do you foster an environment that encourages continual learning? The answer—offering regular training and development opportunities.

Training should be viewed as an investment rather than a cost. When you invest in your employees, they, in turn, invest their enhanced skills and knowledge back into your business. It's a win-win! Plus, it shows your staff that you value their professional growth and are willing to support them.

Don't limit training to technical skills only. Soft skills like communication, leadership, and project management are just as important in the engineering world. Blend a mix of in-house training, external courses, webinars, and workshops. And remember, not all learning comes from formal training. Encourage knowledge sharing sessions among your team—a veteran welder might have nuggets of wisdom to share with a newbie!

Providing Clear Career Paths

Let's face it, no one wants to feel like they're stuck in a dead-end job. Especially not your CNC machinists or welding technicians who crave the thrill of creating and innovating. Providing clear career paths for your employees not only motivates them but also gives them a sense of direction and purpose.

Start by mapping out potential career trajectories within your organisation. These could be vertical moves (promotions), horizontal moves (transfers to different departments or roles), or even diagonal moves (a combination of both). Make sure these paths are transparent and communicated clearly to your employees.

Regularly review these career paths with your employees. Discuss their career goals, their progress, and the steps they need to take to achieve their ambitions. Remember, a career path is not a one-size-fits-all; it should be tailored to each individual's aspirations and abilities.

Supporting Employee Goals

The key to retaining staff in a competitive market is to show that you care about their individual goals and ambitions, not just the company's bottom line. When employees feel that their personal goals are aligned with the company's, they are more likely to stay committed and motivated.

Start by having regular one-on-one meetings with your staff. Use these as an opportunity to understand their career aspirations, what motivates them, and any challenges they might be facing. Then, think about how you can support them in achieving these goals. This could be through training, mentoring, or providing opportunities for them to take on new projects or responsibilities.

Celebrate their achievements, no matter how small. This demonstrates that you recognise their efforts and value their contribution to the company. Also, be flexible and understanding. If an employee wants to pursue further education or needs to adjust their working hours, try to accommodate them as much as possible.

Supporting your employees' goals isn't just about making them feel good—it's about creating a work environment where they can thrive and contribute their best to your business.

In conclusion, fostering career development and progression is crucial in retaining staff in a competitive market. By offering training and development opportunities, providing clear career paths, and supporting employee goals, you can create a workforce that is motivated, committed, and ready to take your manufacturing or engineering business to new heights.

Remember, your employees are your most valuable asset. Invest in them, and they will invest in you.

Maintaining a Healthy Work Environment

Creating a healthy work environment is like maintaining a well-oiled machine. It requires regular checks, constant attention, and prompt action whenever something goes out of sync. In this part, we will delve into three crucial aspects of maintaining a healthy work environment: promoting work-life balance, encouraging team collaboration, and addressing workplace conflicts.

Promoting Work-Life Balance

In the hustle and bustle of the engineering and manufacturing industry, maintaining a healthy work-life balance can often get tossed to the wayside. But you know what? That's a mistake. It's a mistake that can cost you your most valuable asset - your staff. Here's why.

Work-life balance isn't just about ensuring your employees can get home in time for dinner. It's about creating an environment where they can thrive both at work and outside of it, where they can feel fulfilled and motivated to give their best each day. It's about understanding that your staff are not robots, but human beings with lives outside of work.

Encourage your staff to take regular breaks and to use their annual leave. Resist the urge to email them after hours. Consider offering flexible working hours or remote working options. Showing that you care about their wellbeing can make a huge difference in their morale and productivity.

Encouraging Team Collaboration

Picture this – a welding team that works together like a well-oiled machine. They understand each other's strengths, compensate for each other's weaknesses, and can almost predict what the other will do next. That's the power of collaboration, and it's something you definitely want to cultivate in your workplace.

But how do you do that? It starts with creating a culture of openness and transparency. Encourage your team to share their ideas, to communicate openly, and to support each other. Foster a sense of camaraderie through team building activities – these don't have to be grand outings, even casual Friday lunches can do the trick.

Remember, collaboration isn't just about getting your staff to work together. It's about creating an environment where they feel comfortable expressing their viewpoints, where they feel their contributions are valued, and where everyone works towards a common goal.

Addressing Workplace Conflicts

Let's face it - conflicts are inevitable in any workplace. But in the high-pressure environment of the engineering and manufacturing industry, unresolved conflicts can rapidly escalate, affecting morale, productivity, and ultimately, your bottom line.

Addressing workplace conflicts promptly and effectively is crucial. Make it clear that bullying or harassment will not be tolerated. Encourage open communication and ensure your staff feel safe to express their concerns.

When conflicts do arise, don't just sweep them under the carpet. Address them head-on. Listen to all parties involved, mediate if necessary, and work towards a resolution that is fair for everyone. Remember that while conflicts can be challenging, they can also be an opportunity for growth and learning.

Creating a healthy work environment isn't a one-off task, it's a continuous process. It requires you to be proactive, to be aware of what's going on in your workplace, and to take action whenever necessary. It's not always easy, but the rewards – a motivated, engaged, and productive workforce – are definitely worth it. So, roll up your sleeves and get to work on creating the best possible environment for your team. After all, your success as a business owner in the engineering and manufacturing industry hinges on it.

RECAP AND ACTION ITEMS

So there we have it, you've just navigated through the nitty-gritty of retaining staff in a fiercely competitive market. Let's have a quick recap before we jump into the action steps.

We covered how pivotal employee engagement can be for your organisation, digging into the power of regular feedback and recognition, the potency of providing continuous learning opportunities, and the impact of encouraging employee input. We also explored the significance of career development, offering training and development, creating clear career paths, and supporting your employees' personal goals. Lastly, we delved into the importance of a healthy work environment, promoting work-life balance, fostering team collaboration, and addressing workplace conflicts promptly and effectively.

Now, let's break this down into actionable steps:

1. Set in motion a system for frequent feedback and recognition. Make it part of your culture to acknowledge and appreciate good work, and to give constructive feedback where necessary.

2. Develop a learning and development program. Invest in your employees by providing them with opportunities to learn and grow. This could be in the form of on-the-job training, seminars, or even sponsoring further education.

3. Implement an open-door policy. Encourage your employees to voice their thoughts, ideas, and concerns. This will not only make them feel valued but can also bring fresh perspectives to

your business.

4. Establish clear career paths within your organisation. Show your employees there's room for advancement and support them in their journey.

5. Prioritise work-life balance. Encourage your employees to take time off when needed. Remember, a happy, healthy employee is far more productive than a burnt-out one.

6. Foster a collaborative environment. Organise team-building activities or create spaces where employees can interact and unwind.

7. Address workplace conflicts promptly. Don't let minor issues escalate into major problems. Have clear policies in place and ensure they are enforced fairly.

Remember, retaining staff isn't rocket science, but it does require consistent effort and genuine care. Keep these action steps in mind and you'll be well on your way to fostering a workplace that your employees wouldn't dream of leaving. Onwards and upwards!

5

LEVERAGING RECRUITMENT AGENCIES FOR SUCCESS

"Coming together is a beginning, staying together is progress, and working together is success." - Henry Ford

The Role of Recruitment Agencies

Let's dive right in, shall we? As a business owner in the manufacturing or engineering industry, you're probably always on the lookout for ways to streamline your operations and get the best possible results. One area where many businesses can make significant improvements is in their recruitment processes. This is where recruitment agencies come into play.

Outsourcing Recruitment

Think about it - you're an expert in your field, whether that's welding, CNC, or another area of manufacturing or engineering. But are you also an expert in recruitment? Probably not - and that's okay!

Outsourcing recruitment to a specialist agency allows you to focus on what you do best, leaving the job of finding and hiring the best talent to those who have the necessary expertise. It's all about playing to your strengths and letting others play to theirs.

By outsourcing your recruitment, you're not just hiring a service, you're buying time, reducing stress, and most importantly, securing the best talent for your business. You're turning a time-consuming and often frustrating process into a smooth and efficient one. It's a win-win, really.

Accessing Specialist Knowledge

Next on our list is the recruitment agencies' speciality knowledge. They're not just good at what they do, they're experts. They live and breathe recruitment, staying up-to-date on the latest trends, changes in legislation, and best practices.

These agencies understand the specific needs of your industry and the skills and qualifications necessary for each role. They can tap into their extensive network of candidates, many of whom may not be actively seeking a new job but could be persuaded to make a move for the right opportunity.

This specialist knowledge can help you find the best fit for your open positions, even if those roles are highly specialised or difficult to fill. It's like having your own personal talent scout, always on the lookout for the best and brightest in your field.

Saving Time and Resources

Let's not forget about the considerable time and resources that are saved when you outsource your recruitment. Think about the hours spent writing job descriptions, advertising vacancies, sifting through CVs, conducting preliminary interviews, checking references - the list goes on.

By outsourcing these tasks to a recruitment agency, you can free up your internal resources to focus on other, more strategic aspects of your business. It's not just about saving time, but also about using your time more efficiently. After all, time is money, and in business, every penny counts.

Choosing the Right Recruitment Agency

If you're to harness the power of staffing and skyrocket your revenue, you need to ensure that you're choosing the right recruitment agency. This is paramount. It's not just about picking the first name that pops up on your Google search. It's about due diligence and understanding what makes an agency the right fit for your business.

Understanding Agency Specialities

The first thing to remember is that not all agencies are created equal. They have their specialities, their niches. Much like you wouldn't go to a butcher to buy a loaf of bread, you shouldn't go to a general recruitment agency when you need to fill a specialist engineering or manufacturing role.

Imagine trying to find a new CNC operator. You could go with a generalist agency, sure. But you'll likely end up sifting through hundreds of CVs, many of which will be from candidates who have no idea what a CNC machine even is.

On the other hand, a specialist agency will give you a smaller pool of candidates. However, these candidates will all be qualified, experienced and ready to hit the ground running. They'll know their G-code from their M-code. They'll know about toolpaths, speeds, and feeds.

So, before you choose your agency, do your homework. Look at their website, check out their LinkedIn profiles. Do they specialise in your industry? Do they understand the intricacies of your roles? If not, it might be time to look elsewhere.

Checking Agency Track Record

Next up on your recruitment agency checklist is their track record. Just like in any business, past performance is a good indicator of future success.

What's the agency's reputation in the industry? Check out their testimonials, case studies, or any industry awards they've won. Ask around. Word of mouth is still one of the most powerful ways to gauge an agency's reputation.

It's also worth checking out their fill rate. This is the percentage of roles they successfully fill. A high fill rate means they're good at what they do. They know how to match the right candidate to the right role.

Don't forget to consider their retention rate too. It's one thing to fill a role, but it's another thing entirely to fill it with someone who sticks around. A high retention rate is a good sign that they're not just placing anyone, but placing the right one.

Assessing Agency Fit

Last, but certainly not least, is assessing whether the agency is a good fit for your business. This is about more than just their specialities and track record. It's about how they work, their processes, their values.

How do they communicate? Do they prefer email, phone calls, or face-to-face meetings? Do their communication preferences align with yours?

What's their recruitment process? Is it thorough? Do they take the time to understand your business, your culture, your vision? Will they represent your brand well to potential candidates?

And, of course, do their values align with yours? An agency that shares your values will be far more invested in your success. They'll go the extra mile to find the right candidates for your business.

In summary, choosing the right recruitment agency is a crucial step in leveraging staffing for success. It involves understanding the agency's specialities, checking their track record, and assessing whether they're the right fit for your business. Take the time to do this well and you'll be one step closer to skyrocketing your revenue.

Remember, you're not just choosing a supplier. You're choosing a partner. You're choosing someone who will represent your brand and your business to potential candidates. So, choose wisely. Your success depends on it.

Working with Your Recruitment Agency

So, you've nailed down the role of recruitment agencies and even managed to pick one that fits your needs like a well-oiled machine. Now the real work begins. This isn't a "set it and forget it" process. Like any relationship, it requires effort, communication, and, most importantly, a shared vision.

Communicating Your Needs

This isn't about vague requests or throwing around industry jargon. When it comes to communicating with your recruitment agency, specificity is your best friend. Remember, these aren't mind-readers. They're professionals who can help you pinpoint and secure the talent you need to drive your business forward. But to do that, they need to know exactly what you're looking for.

Let's say you're in the market for an experienced CNC machine operator. Instead of simply stating the job title, delve into the details. What specific skills are you looking for? Are there any particular projects or types of machinery they should have experience with? What about certifications or training? The more information you can provide, the better equipped your recruitment agency will be to find candidates who tick all the right boxes.

This isn't a one-time deal, either. As your business evolves, so too will your staffing needs. Keeping the lines of communication open and regularly updating your agency on any changes or new requirements is crucial.

Providing Feedback

If you're not happy with the candidates your recruitment agency is sending your way, don't suffer in silence. Providing feedback is an integral part of the process. If a candidate wasn't a good fit, let your agency know why. Was it a lack of experience? A personality clash? Or perhaps they just didn't mesh well with your company culture?

Likewise, if a candidate was a knockout, share that too. This will help your agency understand what works and what doesn't for your business, enabling them to fine-tune their search and deliver even better results moving forward.

The key here is constructive criticism. This isn't a venting session. It's an opportunity to provide valuable insights that can help your recruitment agency better serve your needs. Remember, they want to find you the perfect candidates just as much as you do.

Building a Long-term Partnership

This isn't a sprint, it's a marathon. Building a fruitful, long-term partnership with your recruitment agency is an investment that can pay serious dividends down the line.

How do you cultivate such a partnership? By treating your agency as an extension of your internal team. This means sharing your business goals, plans for growth, and any potential challenges you foresee. The more they understand about your business, the better equipped they'll be to help you navigate the ever-changing employment landscape.

This also means being open to their expertise. Your recruitment agency is a treasure trove of industry knowledge and insights. They can offer advice on everything from current hiring trends to salary benchmarks and even strategies for retaining top talent.

In essence, building a long-term partnership is about fostering mutual trust and respect. It's about acknowledging that you're in this together and that your success is their success.

Working with a recruitment agency is not just about filling vacancies. It's about leveraging their expertise to cultivate a talented, committed workforce that can propel your business to new heights. So communicate, provide feedback, and invest in building a strong, long-term partnership. The results might just surprise you.

Remember, in the world of engineering and manufacturing, talent isn't just a nice-to-have. It's the engine that drives innovation, efficiency, and ultimately, success. So don't just use your recruitment agency. Work with them, and watch your business thrive.

RECAP AND ACTION ITEMS

Alright, let's wrap this up, shall we? You've learned the ins and outs of recruitment agencies - what they bring to the table, how to pick the right one and how to work with them effectively.

So, let's get to it – it's time to take some action!

Step 1: Evaluate your current recruitment process. Where are the gaps? Where are you wasting time and money? Outsourcing your recruitment could be the game-changer you need. It opens up a world of specialist knowledge that can save you resources and simplify your life.

Step 2: Research agencies and understand their specialities. Not all agencies are created equal. Some might have a killer track record in the manufacturing sector, while others might shine in the world of welding. The trick is to find the one that best suits your needs.

Step 3: Don't just stop at their track record, though. You need to assess whether an agency is a good fit for your company. Are their values aligned with yours? Do they understand your vision? It's about building a partnership, not just hiring a service.

Step 4: Once you've selected an agency, it's all about communication. Be clear about your needs and expectations. Provide feedback consistently. Remember, this is a two-way street, and transparency is key to a successful partnership.

Step 5: Think long-term. Building a solid, lasting relationship with your recruitment agency can lead to consistent success in attracting top talent. You're in this for the long haul, so make sure your agency is too.

And just like that, you're ready to harness the power of staffing and skyrocket your revenue. It's not rocket science – it's just smart business. So, what are you waiting for? Time to get out there and start leveraging recruitment agencies for success!

6

THE FUTURE OF RECRUITMENT IN MANUFACTURING AND ENGINEERING

"The only thing we know about the future is that it will be different."
- Peter Drucker

The Impact of Technology

Let's dive right into it. The world is rapidly evolving, and technology is leading the charge. As a business owner in the manufacturing and engineering industries, you're already harnessing the power of technology to streamline processes and boost productivity. But have you ever stopped to consider how technology could be revolutionising your recruitment process? If not, you're missing out on some serious potential.

Leveraging AI in Recruitment

Artificial Intelligence (AI) isn't just for science fiction films or high-tech labs anymore. It's here, it's now, and it's transforming the way businesses source, screen, and hire talent. Yes, even in manufacturing and engineering.

Imagine a world where you don't need to sift through hundreds of CVs for each position. Instead, an intelligent algorithm does that for you, selecting the most qualified candidates based on your specific criteria. That's AI recruitment for you. It does the heavy lifting, freeing up your time to focus on what you do best – running your business.

AI also helps to remove unconscious bias in the recruitment process. It doesn't care about names, ages, or genders. It only cares about skills, qualifications, and experiences. That's it.

But there's more. AI doesn't just work 9-5. It's always on, always working. This means you're recruiting 24/7, 365 days a year. You're always on the lookout for top talent, even when you're sleeping. How's that for efficiency?

Using Social Media for Sourcing

We live in a connected world, and social media is the glue that binds us together. Facebook, LinkedIn, Twitter – these are more than just platforms for sharing photos or viral memes. They're pools brimming with potential candidates.

But harnessing the power of social media for recruitment isn't about posting a job ad and hoping for the best. It's about engaging with your audience, building your employer brand, and making your company a place people want to work.

Start by sharing content that reflects your company's culture and values. Show off your state-of-the-art CNC machines, or your team of skilled welders in action. Give potential candidates a glimpse of what it's like to work for you.

Next, use social media to open a dialogue. Encourage your followers to ask questions, leave comments, or share their thoughts. The more engaged your audience is, the more likely they are to apply for your jobs.

Remember, social media isn't a one-way street. It's a conversation. And the more you participate in that conversation, the more successful your recruitment efforts will be.

Making Use of Mobile Recruiting

In today's world, almost everyone has a smartphone in their pocket. And they're using those smartphones for more than just calling or texting. They're browsing the web, shopping online, and yes, even job hunting.

So, if your recruitment efforts aren't optimised for mobile, you're potentially missing out on a large pool of candidates. Making your job ads mobile-friendly isn't a luxury, it's a necessity.

But mobile recruiting isn't just about making your job ads look good on a small screen. It's about simplifying the application process. Nobody wants to fill out a lengthy application form on their phone. So keep it short and sweet. Ask for the bare minimum information needed to assess a candidate's suitability for a role. You can always ask for more details later.

In the same vein, consider integrating with popular job search apps. This will make it easier for candidates to find and apply for your jobs, increasing the likelihood of attracting top talent.

Technology is a game-changer in the world of recruitment. By leveraging AI, using social media, and making the most of mobile recruiting, you can streamline your hiring process, reach a wider pool of candidates, and ultimately find the best fit for your manufacturing or engineering business. So, don't fear the future. Embrace it. After all, the future is now.

The Role of Data in Recruitment

Data, data, data. It's not just the buzzword of the 21st century; it is the core of sound, strategic decision-making in any field, including recruitment. It's no longer just about sifting through piles of CVs or having a 'gut feeling' about a candidate. It's about leveraging data to make informed, strategic recruitment decisions.

Let's dive in to how you can use data effectively in your recruitment process.

Using Analytics for Decision-making

Imagine having the ability to predict the success of a potential hire before they even start. Sounds like science fiction, right? Well, it's not. Welcome to the world of predictive analytics.

Predictive analytics utilises statistical techniques like data mining, predictive modelling, and machine learning to analyse current and historical facts to make predictions about future outcomes. In recruitment, it can help you identify the best candidates, predict future hiring needs, and even foresee potential retention issues.

For instance, let's say you're looking to hire a CNC machinist. By using predictive analytics, you can identify key characteristics of successful CNC machinists in your company. You can then use this information to screen potential candidates and identify those who are most likely to succeed in the role.

In addition, predictive analytics can also help you identify potential retention issues. For example, if your data shows that CNC machinists who work late shifts are more likely to leave within the first year, you can use this information to adjust your shift scheduling or provide additional support to these employees.

Tracking Recruitment Metrics

In the world of recruitment, knowledge is power, and the best way to gain knowledge is by tracking your recruitment metrics. These can include time to hire, cost per hire, source of hire, and quality of hire, among others.

Let's take the 'time to hire' metric, for instance. If it's taking you an average of 60 days to fill a position when the industry standard is 30, you know there's a problem. You're not only losing productivity due to the vacant position, but you're also likely losing top candidates to competitors who can move faster.

Similarly, if your 'cost per hire' is sky-high, it's a sign that your recruitment process may be inefficient. By tracking this metric, you can identify where you're spending the most money and take steps to streamline the process and reduce costs.

Predicting Future Hiring Needs

In the fast-paced world of manufacturing and engineering, being able to anticipate future hiring needs can give you a competitive edge.

This is where data comes in. By analysing trends in your industry, changes in your workforce, and your company's growth plans, you can predict future hiring needs and start sourcing candidates before you even have a vacancy. This not only reduces your time to hire but also gives you a larger pool of candidates to choose from.

For example, if your data shows an increasing demand for welding professionals in your industry and you're planning to expand your operations in the next year, you can anticipate the need for more welders and start sourcing candidates now.

Data can also help you identify potential skills gaps in your workforce. If your data shows that a significant number of your engineers are nearing retirement age, you can start planning for this by recruiting younger engineers or offering training to your existing workforce.

The use of data in recruitment is not just a trend or a passing fad. It's a strategic approach that can help you make informed decisions, streamline your recruitment process, and ultimately, secure the best talent for your company. It's time to embrace the power of data and let it drive your recruitment strategy.

Preparing for Future Skills Needs

As a business owner in the manufacturing and engineering industries, you've probably heard the phrase "the only constant is change". This is particularly true in your field, where technological advancements and industry shifts can significantly impact the skills your workforce needs to stay competitive. So, how can you prepare for these future skills needs? It starts with keeping up with industry trends, planning for skills shortages, and investing in employee training.

Keeping up with Industry Trends

The first step towards preparing for future skills needs is staying abreast of trends in the manufacturing and engineering industries. This can be a game-changer; if you know what's coming down the pipeline, you can take steps to ensure your team is ready to meet these challenges head-on.

So, how can you keep up with industry trends? There's no shortage of resources available. Websites like Engineering.com and Manufacturing.net provide daily news updates and in-depth articles on the latest industry trends. Trade shows and conferences can also be goldmines of information. Not only do they provide the opportunity to learn about new technologies and methods, but they also offer the chance to network with other industry professionals who may have insights to share.

Planning for Skills Shortages

Once you've identified the trends shaping your industry, the next step is to plan for any potential skills shortages. This isn't always an easy task; it requires a forward-thinking mindset and the ability to accurately assess your current workforce's capabilities.

Start by conducting a skills gap analysis. This involves identifying the skills your workforce currently possesses and comparing them to the skills they'll need in the future. The 'gap' between the two is your skills shortage.

Once you know where the gaps are, you can begin to develop a plan to fill them. This could involve recruitment strategies to bring in new talent, or it could mean upskilling your current workforce. The important thing is to have a plan in place that can adapt to changing needs.

Investing in Employee Training

Investing in employee training is another crucial element in preparing for future skills needs. It's a proactive approach that not only helps fill skills gaps but also boosts employee engagement and loyalty.

A robust training programme can take many forms, depending on your specific needs. For instance, you might choose to offer in-house training sessions on new technologies or techniques. Alternatively, you might partner with a vocational school or community college to provide continuing education opportunities for your employees.

Investing in employee training also includes creating a culture of learning within your organisation. Encourage curiosity and innovation. Make it clear that you value continuous learning and that you're committed to helping your employees grow and develop in their roles.

Remember, the goal is not just to prepare for future skills needs, but to build a resilient, adaptable workforce that can navigate whatever changes come your way.

Summary

In the fast-paced world of manufacturing and engineering, preparing for future skills needs is not just a nice-to-have; it's a necessity. By keeping up with industry trends, planning for skills shortages, and investing in employee training, you're not only setting your business up for future success – you're also ensuring that your workforce is equipped to meet the challenges of tomorrow.

In the words of legendary author Tim Ferris, "The future belongs to those who learn more skills and combine them in creative ways". So, go forth and prepare for future skills needs. Your business – and your employees – will thank you.

RECAP AND ACTION ITEMS

Phew! We've covered a lot of ground in this chapter, haven't we? Let's summarise and get you ready to take action.

First off, technology is revolutionising the recruitment game. AI is not only streamlining but also enhancing the hiring process. It's time to wrap your head around this and leverage the technology to your advantage. Then there's social media. It's no longer just a platform for cat videos and holiday snaps, it's a goldmine of potential hires. Tap into it. And let's not forget mobile recruiting. With more people using their phones for everything, you'd be missing out if you're not optimising your recruitment for mobile.

Next, we talked about data. It's the new oil, they say, and it's definitely true for recruitment. Analytics can help you make better decisions, tracking recruitment metrics can give you insights into what's working and what's not, and predicting future hiring needs can save you from scrambling when the need arises.

Finally, keep your eyes on the future. Stay updated with industry trends, plan for potential skills shortages and invest in training your employees. Your business is as good as your team, and upskilling them is a sure-fire way to stay ahead of the game.

So, what's next? Here are some action items for you:

1. Research AI tools that could be suitable for your recruitment process. Try a few out, and see what works best for you

2. Create a social media strategy to attract talent. Who are you trying to reach and where are they hanging out online?

3. Make sure your job ads and application processes are mobile-friendly

4. Start tracking your recruitment metrics. What gets measured gets managed, remember?

5. Use data to predict your future hiring needs. Begin planning now

6. Stay updated with industry trends. Subscribe to the relevant newsletters, attend webinars or industry events

7. Develop a plan to deal with any potential skills shortages. Do you need to hire, or can you train your existing team?8. Invest in employee training. What skills will your team need in the future?

There you have it. Now, it's time to take action. Remember, the future of recruitment in manufacturing and engineering is in your hands. Let's make it count!

7

OVERCOMING RECRUITMENT CHALLENGES

"**Great things in business are never done by one person; they're done by a team of people.**" - Steve Jobs

Dealing with Skills Shortages

Hey there, you. Don't let that frown line your face just because you're grappling with a skills shortage in your company. It's not an uncommon problem in the engineering and manufacturing industry. You're not alone. But, it's essential to handle it effectively to prevent it from stifling your company's growth. This chapter is your blueprint to overcoming the skills shortages hurdle. We'll talk about upskilling your current staff, attracting diverse candidates, and partnering with educational institutions.

Upskilling Current Staff

Let's start with the talent you already have in-house. Upskilling your current staff is a no-brainer. It's about taking the skills your team already possesses and cranking them up a notch. It's an investment in human capital that can reap substantial benefits for your business.

Start by identifying the skills gaps in your company. Maybe your welding team needs to learn a new technique, or your CNC operators could benefit from a training course on the latest software. Once you've identified the areas that need improvement, it's time to put a training plan into action.

Training doesn't necessarily mean sending your staff off to expensive courses. Look at on-the-job training, mentoring and online resources. The internet is a treasure trove of tutorials and webinars that your team can tap into. Make learning a part of your company culture.

Remember, upskilling isn't a one-and-done deal. It's an ongoing process. Keep the lines of communication open and encourage your staff to take the initiative to learn new skills. When they see that you're invested in their growth, they'll be more likely to stick around and help your company flourish.

Attracting Diverse Candidates

Now, let's move on to bringing new blood into your company. The world is full of different people, each with their unique set of skills and experiences. Embracing diversity isn't just about ticking a box; it's about enriching your company with a myriad of perspectives.

To attract diverse candidates, you first need to analyse your job descriptions. Are they written in a way that encourages people from all walks of life to apply? If not, it's time to jazz them up. Highlight the equal opportunities within your company and the value you place on diversity.

Next, consider where you're advertising your vacancies. If you're only posting on the same old job boards, it's time to branch out. Leverage social media, attend job fairs, and reach out to organisations that cater to diverse groups.

Finally, examine your company culture. Do you have an inclusive environment that respects and values individual differences? If not, it's time to make some changes. A company that celebrates diversity is a company that people want to be a part of.

Partnering with Educational Institutions

To overcome skills shortages, you'll need to take a long-term view. That's where partnering with educational institutions comes in. By creating strong ties with schools, colleges, and universities, you can ensure a steady influx of skilled workers into your business.

Start by identifying the institutions that offer courses related to your industry. Then, establish a relationship with them. Offer to provide guest lectures or host field trips to your facility. You could even sponsor scholarships or internships.

By partnering with educational institutions, you not only gain access to a pool of potential employees, but you also have the chance to influence the curriculum. This way, you can ensure that students are learning the skills that your industry needs.

Overcoming skills shortages isn't easy, but it's not impossible either. With a strategic approach to upskilling your current staff, attracting diverse candidates, and partnering with educational institutions, you can turn this challenge into an opportunity. Remember, it's not about filling roles; it's about building a team that will drive your company forward. You have the power to do this. So, let's get to it.

Reducing Time to Hire

You know as well as anyone that time is money, especially when it comes to filling vacant positions in your business. The longer a role sits empty, the more productivity and potential revenue you're losing. Let's dive into how to reduce your time to hire.

Streamlining Recruitment Processes

The first thing you need to do is take a long, hard look at your current recruitment process. Is it efficient? Is it effective? Or is it more like a maze, full of dead ends and unnecessary detours that are slowing things down?

Streamlining your recruitment process is all about simplifying and speeding up the steps it takes to go from vacancy to hire. For instance, consider implementing a structured interview process. This means asking the same set of questions to every candidate, which can help you quickly compare and contrast their responses. It also eliminates any potential bias and ensures a fair process for all.

Another way to streamline is to delegate. Maybe you're trying to do too much yourself. If you have a trusted team, delegate some of the recruitment tasks to them. Sharing the load can speed up the process and help ensure you don't miss potential good hires because you're stretched too thin.

Leveraging Technology

In this digital age, technology is your friend, and it can be a game-changer when it comes to reducing your time to hire.

Consider investing in applicant tracking systems (ATS). An ATS can help you manage applications, screen resumes, and even set up automatic responses to candidates, saving you a ton of time.

Another technology to consider is video interviewing software. Instead of scheduling and conducting time-consuming in-person interviews, you can have candidates record their responses to your questions at their convenience. You can then review the responses when it suits you best. This not only saves you time but also widens your candidate pool by removing geographical barriers.

Finally, social media and LinkedIn can be used to spread the word about your vacancies, attract potential candidates and quickly get an understanding of their skills and experience.

Improving Candidate Communication

Communication plays a key role in how quickly you can fill a vacancy. If candidates are left in the dark, waiting for weeks to hear back about their application or interview, they're likely to lose interest and move on to other opportunities.

Acknowledge applications as soon as they arrive, set clear expectations about the process and follow through. Let applicants know when they can expect to hear from you, and stick to it. If there are delays, be upfront about them. Transparency builds trust and keeps candidates engaged.

Also, don't hesitate to pick up the phone. While email and text are great for quick updates, a phone call can make a candidate feel valued and give you the chance to gauge their continued interest.

Incorporate these strategies into your recruitment process, and you'll be well on your way to reducing your time to hire. Remember, every day a position remains vacant is a day of lost productivity and potential revenue. By streamlining the recruitment process, leveraging technology, and improving candidate communication, you'll fill those vacancies quicker and keep your business running at full steam.

And remember, reducing time to hire doesn't just mean filling a vacancy quickly. It also means finding the right person for the job, someone who will add value to your company in the long term. So don't rush – be efficient, be smart, and you'll find the right balance.

Managing Hiring Costs

The task of managing hiring costs is not unlike walking a tightrope. You're trying to balance the cost and quality of new hires, invest in retention, and make smart hiring decisions. This might feel like a juggling act on a high wire, but it's not as daunting as it might seem. Let's dive in, shall we?

Balancing Cost and Quality

First things first, let's address the elephant in the room - the cost vs quality conundrum. Lowering hiring costs doesn't mean hiring the cheapest candidate. It's about hiring the right candidate for the right price.

Consider the costs of a poor hire - low productivity, decreased morale, additional training, and potentially, the cost of replacing them. Suddenly, that "cheap" hire isn't so economical after all. So, how do you strike that elusive balance?

Start by re-evaluating your job descriptions. Are they attracting the right type of candidates? Are they clear on the skills and experience required? A well-written job description can act like a filter, reducing the number of unsuitable applicants and saving you time and money in the recruitment process.

Next, take a look at your interview process. Can it be streamlined or improved to better identify top talent? Perhaps you could incorporate practical assignments or tests that directly relate to the tasks they'll be performing on the job.

Finally, don't forget to negotiate. Salary negotiation is a normal part of the hiring process. It's a two-way street where both parties aim to reach an agreement that's fair and beneficial to both sides.

Investing in Retention

Now, let's pivot to retention, because keeping your current staff happy and engaged can significantly reduce your hiring costs. After all, you're not just hiring for today - you're hiring for the future of your company.

Investing in your current staff can take many forms. It might be providing opportunities for professional development or upskilling, implementing a rewards or recognition program, or simply offering competitive salaries and benefits. Even small gestures can make a big difference.

Remember, when your employees feel valued and see opportunities for growth, they're less likely to look elsewhere. Plus, a positive work environment can turn your employees into your best recruiters, attracting top talent to your company.

Making Smart Hiring Decisions

Smart hiring decisions are about more than just filling an open position. It's about finding the right person who will add value to your business and fit into your company culture.

One way to make smart hiring decisions is to think long term. Instead of just looking at the skills and experience a candidate has now, consider their potential for growth. Do they have a willingness to learn? Are they adaptable? These qualities can be invaluable in the ever-changing landscape of the manufacturing and engineering industries.

Another strategy is to consider the total cost of hiring, not just the salary. This includes the cost of recruitment, onboarding, training, and any potential downtime while the new hire gets up to speed.

Lastly, don't rush. A rushed decision can lead to a poor hire, which can end up costing you more in the long run.

Managing hiring costs is not just about reducing expenses. It's about investing wisely, making smart decisions, and creating a workforce that will drive your business forward. Because at the end of the day, your staff is not just an expense - they're an investment in the future of your company.

So, as you navigate the tightrope of hiring costs, remember to keep your balance. Invest in quality and retention, make smart decisions, and you'll not only survive the high wire act, you'll master it.

RECAP AND ACTION ITEMS:

Alright, you've navigated the tricky terrain of recruitment, filled skills gaps, reduced hiring time, and managed costs. Let's now distil what you've learned into clear, actionable steps.

First up, dealing with skills shortages. Remember, upskilling your current staff is crucial. Investing in your current team not only bridges the skills gap but also increases staff morale and loyalty. Set up regular training sessions and provide opportunities for them to learn and grow.

Don't forget to attract diverse candidates. A diverse workforce brings in a wide range of skills, perspectives, and ideas. Connect with different communities, attend career fairs, and ensure your job ads are inclusive.

Lastly, partner with educational institutions. They're a goldmine of fresh talents. Sponsor events, offer internships, and create apprenticeship programmes to cultivate a steady supply of skilled workers.

Next, reducing time to hire. Streamline your recruitment processes. Simplify job descriptions, get clear on what you're looking for, and shorten the interview process.

Leverage technology. Use recruitment software to automate and speed up tasks. There are plenty of tools out there that can make your life easier.

Don't underestimate the power of communication. Keep candidates informed throughout the process. It shows respect and keeps top talents engaged.

Lastly, managing hiring costs. Balance cost and quality. Yes, hiring can be expensive, but remember, you get what you pay for. Don't skimp on quality.

Invest in retention. It's more cost-effective to keep a great employee than to hire a new one. Provide a positive work environment and competitive benefits.

Finally, make smart hiring decisions. Consider the long-term potential of candidates, not just their immediate skills.

Now, it's time for action. Take these insights, apply them, and start overcoming your recruitment challenges. You've got this!

8

BUILDING A HIGH-PERFORMING TEAM

"Alone we can do so little; together we can do so much." – **Helen Keller**

The Importance of Team Dynamics

In the fast-paced world of engineering and manufacturing, you know as well as anyone that a well-oiled machine is only as good as its individual components. The same principle applies to your team. Ensuring your team functions as a high-performing unit is integral to your business's overall success. That's where the magic of team dynamics comes in.

Encouraging Team Collaboration

We've all heard the phrase, "two heads are better than one", haven't we? In the world of welding and CNC, this couldn't be more accurate. Encouraging collaboration within your team not only facilitates the sharing of ideas and skills but also fosters a sense of unity and mutual respect.

Think about the last time you worked on a project alone. It was tough, right? Now imagine that same project with a team of experienced professionals, each contributing their unique skills and perspectives. The difference is palpable.

But encouraging collaboration isn't just about assembling a group of individuals. It's about fostering an environment where everyone feels comfortable sharing their ideas and insights. This might involve implementing regular team meetings, brainstorming sessions, or even social events outside of work hours. Remember, collaboration is not a one-time event, but a continuous process that should be woven into the fabric of your company culture.

Managing Team Conflicts

Now, let's get real for a moment. Where there's a team, there's bound to be conflict. It's a natural part of any group dynamic. However, it's how you manage these conflicts that can make or break your team's performance.

Conflicts can arise from a myriad of sources – differing opinions, personality clashes, or even just the stress of a looming deadline. They can be disruptive, sure, but they can also be a catalyst for growth and development if handled correctly.

The key to managing team conflicts effectively is to encourage open and honest communication. This means providing a safe space for team members to express their thoughts and concerns without fear of retribution. It also means leading by example – showing your team that it's okay to disagree, as long as it's done in a respectful and constructive manner.

Consider implementing conflict resolution strategies, such as mediation or team-building exercises. These can help diffuse tension and foster a sense of unity within your team. Remember, a team that can navigate conflict together is a team that can weather any storm.

Promoting Positive Behaviours

Finally, let's talk about promoting positive behaviours. In the world of engineering and manufacturing, it's easy to get caught up in the technicalities and forget about the human element. But it's this human element – the attitudes, behaviours, and values of your team members – that can truly make or break your team's performance.

Promoting positive behaviours is about more than just rewarding good work (although that's certainly part of it). It's about cultivating a positive work environment where team members feel valued and respected. It's about setting clear expectations and providing constructive feedback. Most importantly, it's about leading by example.

Consider implementing a recognition program to reward team members for their hard work and dedication. Encourage open communication and transparency in all aspects of your business. Foster a culture of respect, where everyone's ideas and contributions are valued. And, of course, lead by example –

show your team the kind of behaviour you expect through your own actions.

In conclusion, understanding and nurturing the dynamics within your team is key to building a high-performing unit. By encouraging collaboration, effectively managing conflicts, and promoting positive behaviours, you can create a team that's not only productive but also engaged, motivated, and ready to tackle any challenge that comes their way. So, here's to your team – the heart and soul of your business.

Developing Leadership Skills

In the world of manufacturing and engineering, the power of leadership cannot be underestimated. It's not just about being the boss - it's about inspiring, motivating, and guiding your team to reach their full potential. Let's delve into the three key areas you should focus on to develop leadership skills within your team.

Training and Development

Imagine having a team so well-equipped with skills, they can handle just about any challenge that comes their way. Now, this isn't a far-off dream – it's entirely possible with the right training and development.

As you know, in the manufacturing and engineering industries, technological advancements are the order of the day. New software, tools, and methodologies are continually being developed. So, your team's ability to adapt and learn these new skills is key to staying ahead in the game.

Consider implementing regular training sessions - be it on-site, online, or a mix of both. Don't just focus on technical skills, though. Soft skills, like communication, problem-solving, and critical thinking, are equally important.

And remember, training isn't a one-time thing. It's an ongoing process that should be adapted as your industry evolves. Make it a point to review your training programmes periodically and update them as needed.

Encouraging Leadership Behaviours

Leadership isn't just about being at the top of the hierarchy. It's about taking responsibility, making decisions, and guiding the team towards common goals.

Encourage your team members to take on leadership roles within their scope of work. This could be as simple as leading a project or taking charge of a new initiative. The idea is to give them a taste of leadership, to allow them to experience the challenges and rewards it brings.

Recognise and reward those who step up and show leadership behaviours. This will not only motivate them to continue, but it will also inspire others to follow suit.

But remember, leadership isn't about creating mini versions of yourself. It's about helping each team member develop their unique leadership style. Provide them with the necessary support and guidance, but allow them the freedom to lead in their way.

Providing Leadership Opportunities

Finally, providing opportunities for leadership is crucial. This might seem daunting at first, but it's an essential step in cultivating a team of leaders.

Start by identifying potential leaders within your team. Look for those with the drive, initiative, and aptitude for leadership. Once you've found your potential leaders, give them opportunities to shine. This could be in the form of a promotion, a new project, or even a chance to lead a team meeting.

It's important, however, to ensure that these opportunities are available to all team members, not just a select few. Encourage your team to step up and take on leadership roles, even if it's outside their comfort zone.

Remember, every team member has the potential to be a leader – they just need the right opportunity to show it.

The key to developing leadership skills is continuous effort and encouragement. It's about fostering an environment where leadership is valued and nurtured. By focusing on training and development, encouraging leadership behaviours, and providing leadership opportunities, you can build a team of high-performing leaders.

After all, leadership isn't just about having a title – it's about taking action, inspiring others, and driving success. So, take the time to develop your team's leadership skills – it's a sure-fire way to skyrocket your revenue and ensure the success of your business.

Creating a Culture of Excellence

Let's dive straight in. Building a successful team is one thing, maintaining a culture of excellence is another. And trust me, it's not a walk in the park. But, by setting high standards, recognising and rewarding performance, and encouraging continuous improvement, you can create a culture that thrives on excellence.

Setting High Standards

High standards are the backbone of a culture of excellence. It's not just about having an expectation for good results; it's about setting the bar high enough that your team must stretch to reach it. This is the part where you push your team to step out of their comfort zones and challenge themselves.

Now, you might think, "Isn't that a bit harsh?" But let me tell you this - great things never came from comfort zones. So, how do you set high standards? It's all about clarity and consistency. Ensure your team knows exactly what is expected of them. But remember, high standards should be realistic and achievable. Otherwise, you risk setting your team up for failure and disappointment.

In your engineering or manufacturing business, your high

standards might mean delivering projects on time, maintaining a zero-defect policy, or ensuring safety protocols are adhered to no matter what. Whatever your standards, communicate them clearly and consistently to your team.

Recognising and Rewarding Performance

Recognising and rewarding performance is a crucial part of creating a culture of excellence. Why? Because recognition encourages repeat behaviour. When you acknowledge your team's efforts and achievements, they feel valued and appreciated. And guess what? They'll want to do it again.

Recognition isn't just about a pat on the back or a 'well done' email. It's about genuine appreciation for the effort your team puts in. Don't underestimate the power of a simple thank you. But of course, tangible rewards like bonuses or promotions can be powerful motivators too.

Create a recognition culture where every team member, from your welders to your CNC operators, feels their contributions are valued. And remember to celebrate both individual and team achievements. This not only boosts morale but also fosters a sense of unity and camaraderie among your team.

Encouraging Continuous Improvement

The journey to excellence is never-ending. There's always room for improvement, always a way to do things better, faster, or more efficiently. That's why encouraging continuous improvement is key to maintaining a culture of excellence.

So, how do you encourage continuous improvement? Here's a hint: it's not about pushing your team to work harder. It's about fostering a mindset of constant learning and growth. Encourage your team to seek feedback, to learn from their mistakes, and to continually look for ways to improve their skills and processes.

In the world of engineering and manufacturing, continuous improvement might mean staying abreast of the latest technology, refining workflows for efficiency, or investing in ongoing training and development for your team. Remember, improvement is a journey, not a destination.

All in all, creating a culture of excellence is about setting high standards, recognising and rewarding performance, and encouraging continuous improvement. It's about fostering an environment where your team is motivated to give their best, to keep learning and growing, and to strive for excellence in everything they do.

It's not easy, and it won't happen overnight. But trust me, the results are worth it. A culture of excellence leads to a high-performing team, and a high-performing team leads to skyrocketing revenues for your business. So, what are you waiting for? Start building your culture of excellence today.

RECAP AND ACTION ITEMS:

Alright, you've journeyed through the maze of creating a high-performing team. You've delved into the intricacies of team dynamics, honed leadership skills and cultivated a culture of excellence. Now it's time to put those insights into action.

Let's start with your team dynamics. You want to foster collaboration, manage conflicts, and promote positivity. But how? Start with a simple team meeting. Discuss projects openly, encourage innovative ideas, and don't forget to celebrate team achievements. For conflicts, remember, they're inevitable. But it's how you handle them that matters. Open communication and impartiality are your best tools. And positivity? It's contagious. Lead by example, and your team will follow.

On to leadership skills. You've got to train, encourage, and provide opportunities. Start with a leadership development programme tailored to your industry's needs. Encourage initiative, delegate responsibilities, and always appreciate the extra efforts. Remember, a leader isn't born overnight. It's a journey that needs patience and persistence.

The culture of excellence. It's not a lofty ideal, but a way of life in your organisation. Begin by setting high standards. Not unreachable, but challenging enough to push your team's limits. Recognise and reward performance, both big and small. A simple thank you or a pat on the back goes a long way. And finally, encourage continuous improvement. It's not about being perfect; it's about being better than yesterday.

Now, it's over to you. It might seem like a lot, but take one step at a time. Remember, Rome wasn't built in a day, and neither will your high-performing team. Start small, iterate, learn, and keep moving forward. Your business depends on your team, and it's time to harness their potential. Because at the end of the day, it's not just about skyrocketing your revenue; it's about creating an environment where everyone thrives. And that, my friend, is the true measure of success.

9

THE ROLE OF HR IN RECRUITMENT AND RETENTION

"You don't build a business – You build people – And then people build the business" – Zig Ziglar

Building a Strong HR Team

Imagine this: you've got your competitive product, your state-of-the-art manufacturing facility, and your cutting-edge CNC machines. You're poised to take the engineering world by storm. But there's one crucial element missing. The team. Specifically, your Human Resources (HR) team. They're the backbone of any successful business, engineering or otherwise.

Let's break this down into three key steps to build a solid HR team: Hiring HR professionals, Training and development, and Encouraging HR innovation.

Hiring HR Professionals

First thing's first, you need to bring the right people on board. Now, you might be thinking, "I know how to hire engineers, but HR professionals? That's a whole different ball game." But don't sweat it. It's all about finding people who understand your vision and can help bring it to life.

You want people who are experts in their field. Folks who understand the ins and outs of employment law, who can navigate the complexities of employee benefits, and who can handle difficult conversations with tact and diplomacy. But more than that, you want people who get your industry.

In the engineering world, this means finding HR professionals who understand the unique challenges your employees face. The rigours of a welding shop. The precision required in CNC machining. The pressure of meeting tight project deadlines.

Finding these individuals may seem like searching for a needle in a haystack. But they're out there. Use industry-specific job boards, tap into your network, and don't be afraid to headhunt. After all, you're not just hiring an HR professional. You're hiring a crucial member of your team.

Training and Development

Once you've got your HR dream team in place, it's time to focus on training and development. This isn't a one-off process. It's ongoing. The world of HR is constantly evolving, with new laws, regulations, and best practices emerging all the time. Your HR team needs to stay up to date, and that means regular training and development.

Now, this doesn't have to be a chore. In fact, it can be a powerful tool for team building and morale boosting. Encourage a culture of learning within your HR team. Make it clear that their professional growth is a priority for you.

This could take the form of formal training courses, online webinars, or industry conferences. Or it could be as simple as setting aside time each week for your team to read up on the latest HR trends and developments.

Remember, training and development isn't just about ticking boxes. It's about giving your HR team the tools they need to do their job effectively, and to keep your business on the cutting edge of HR practice.

Encouraging HR Innovation

Finally, let's talk about innovation. In the engineering world, innovation is the name of the game. It's what keeps you ahead of the competition, and it's what drives your business forward. But innovation isn't just for the shop floor. It's just as important in HR.

Encouraging HR innovation means fostering a culture where new ideas are not just welcomed, but actively encouraged. It means being open to new ways of doing things, and not being afraid to shake things up.

Start by creating an environment where your HR team feels comfortable sharing their ideas. This could be through regular brainstorming sessions, suggestion boxes, or just an open-door policy.

Then, when those ideas come in, take them seriously. Give them the consideration they deserve, and be willing to try new things. It might not all work out, but that's okay. Innovation is about taking risks, and not being afraid of failure.

So there you have it. Building a strong HR team isn't just about hiring the right people. It's about investing in their development, and fostering a culture of innovation. It's about recognising that HR is more than just a support function. It's a crucial part of your business strategy.

Remember, in the world of engineering, your people are your greatest asset. And your HR team is the key to unlocking their potential.

HR Policies and Procedures

When it comes to HR, policies and procedures are the backbone of your operation, the framework that holds everything together. They're the rules of the game, setting the standards and expectations for your team. But they're not just about keeping everyone in line, they're also about fostering a positive, productive work environment where everyone feels valued and respected.

Developing Effective Policies

The first step towards creating effective HR policies is to understand your business needs. What are the goals of your company? What kind of culture do you want to foster? These questions will guide the development of your policies. It's not about creating a set of rules for the sake of having rules, but rather about supporting the overall vision and mission of your business.

Start by outlining the key areas you need to cover. This may include attendance, conduct, compensation, benefits, performance management, safety, and confidentiality to name a few. Make sure you also have policies in place that address diversity and inclusion, harassment and discrimination, and employee rights and responsibilities.

When drafting your policies, ensure they are clear, concise, and easy to understand. Avoid jargon or overly complex language. Remember, these policies are for your staff, so they need to be comprehensible to everyone, not just the HR team. They should be fair, consistent, and non-discriminatory.

It's also important to involve your employees in the policy-making process. After all, they're the ones who will be affected by these policies. Getting their input can help ensure that the policies are practical, relevant, and well-received.

Ensuring Legal Compliance

Legal compliance is a critical aspect of HR policies and procedures. It's not just about avoiding lawsuits, it's about protecting your employees and your business. In the UK, you have to comply with various employment laws such as the Employment Rights Act, Equality Act, and Health and Safety at Work Act.

Familiarize yourself with these laws and ensure your policies are in line with them. This isn't just a one-time thing, as employment laws can change often. Regularly review and update your policies to stay compliant.

It's also worthwhile to seek legal counsel when developing or revising your policies. They can help you navigate the complexities of the law and ensure that you're on the right track.

Communicating Policies to Staff

Having the best policies in the world won't mean a thing if your staff aren't aware of them. Communication is key. You need to ensure that your policies are easily accessible to all employees. This could be through an employee handbook, a dedicated section on your company intranet, or regular emails.

But don't just stop at making your policies accessible. Take the time to explain them. Hold training sessions or workshops where you go through the policies in detail, explaining what they mean and how they apply to your employees. This is particularly important for new hires, who may be unfamiliar with your workplace culture and expectations.

Also, remember that communication is a two-way street. Encourage your staff to ask questions and provide feedback on your policies. This can help you identify any areas of confusion or concern, and make necessary adjustments to your policies.

In conclusion, HR policies and procedures play a vital role in the success of your business. They help set the tone for your workplace culture, protect your business from legal issues, and ensure that your staff know what is expected of them. By developing effective policies, ensuring legal compliance, and effectively communicating these policies to your staff, you can create a productive, respectful, and successful work environment.

HR's Role in Employee Engagement

The heart and soul of your business are your employees. They're the ones on the front lines, welding, operating CNC machines, ensuring your products and services are top-notch. But how do you keep these invaluable employees engaged and committed to your business? The answer is simple: your HR team.

Conducting Engagement Surveys

Engagement surveys are the magnifying glass through which you can examine the satisfaction and engagement levels of your employees. These aren't your run-of-the-mill questionnaires packed with a bunch of "yes or no" questions. These are comprehensive, thought-provoking questionnaires designed to give you a deep understanding of your employees' perspectives.

Think of it this way, you need to know if your employees are feeling like a well-oiled machine part of your business or if they're feeling like a rusty cog just waiting to be replaced. And for this, asking the right questions is critical.

These surveys can pinpoint areas where your company excels and where it stumbles. They could expose a lack of training, a need for better equipment, or a desire for more recognition. But remember, these surveys are only as good as the action you take after you've gathered the responses.

Implementing Engagement Strategies

Now that you know what your employees are thinking, it's time to take action. Your HR team should be like a strategic command centre, developing and implementing engagement strategies based on the insights drawn from the surveys.

Maybe your CNC operators need more training on the latest equipment, or your welders feel underappreciated and want more recognition for their hard work. Whatever the case may be, your HR team should be ready to roll out initiatives to address these concerns, whether it's a new training program, an employee recognition scheme, or something as simple as a monthly staff lunch.

These strategies should be tailored to your employees' needs and preferences. There's no point in implementing a fancy new employee portal if your staff would rather have face-to-face meetings.

Monitoring Engagement Levels

Implementing strategies is one thing, but how do you know if they are actually working? This is where monitoring comes in. Your HR team should continuously keep an eye on engagement levels to ensure that the strategies they've implemented are having the desired effect.

This could be through follow-up surveys, one-on-one meetings, or simply by walking around the shop floor and chatting with your employees. After all, engagement isn't a one-and-done deal. It's a continuous process that requires constant attention and tweaking.

For example, you might find that after implementing a new training program, your CNC operators are more confident and productive. Or, you might find that your welders aren't responding to the new recognition scheme as you'd hoped.

In both cases, your HR team should be ready to respond, either by reinforcing successful strategies or rethinking those that aren't hitting the mark.

Remember, your employees are the lifeblood of your business. Their engagement and satisfaction can directly impact the quality of your products, your customer satisfaction, and ultimately, your bottom line. So, invest in your HR team, give them the tools they need to monitor and improve employee engagement, and watch as your business thrives.

In the end, a high-performing, engaged workforce isn't just

good for business, it's good for everyone. It creates a positive work environment where everyone feels valued and appreciated. And when your employees feel like this, they're more likely to go the extra mile for you and your customers.

After all, as you well know, in the world of manufacturing and engineering, every little bit counts. So, why not make sure that every single employee is fully engaged and ready to give their best? Trust me, your bottom line will thank you for it.

RECAP AND ACTION ITEMS

Alright, let's wrap this up. You now understand the vital role of HR in recruitment and retention within your manufacturing or engineering business. Building a strong HR team, developing effective policies and procedures, and engaging employees are critical components of HR's role in your organization.

So, what's next? What do you need to do?

First, focus on building a robust HR team. Not just any team, but a team of HR professionals that understand your industry. Invest in their training and development. Encourage them to come up with innovative ideas. Remember, your HR team is as strong as its weakest link. Make them your partners in driving your business success.

Next, develop effective HR policies and procedures. This is where the rubber meets the road. Your policies should be clear, straightforward, and compliant with all legal requirements. Communication is key here. Make sure everyone in the team knows and understands these policies.

Now, let's talk about employee engagement. This is the secret sauce to retaining your top talent. Listen to your employees. Conduct engagement surveys to get their feedback. Implement engagement strategies that resonate with them. And don't forget to monitor their engagement levels. It's not a one-off thing, it's a continuous process.

Finally, remember that HR is not a siloed function. It is the backbone of your organization. It has the power to attract, retain, and engage the best talent in your industry. Use this power wisely.

Now, it's time for action. Start by assessing your current HR team and practices. What areas need improvement? What are you doing well? Then, create a plan to address these areas.

Remember, change doesn't happen overnight. But with the right HR team, policies and procedures, and engagement strategies, you'll be on your way to harnessing the power of staffing, retaining talent, and skyrocketing your revenue.

So, get to it. Your business success depends on it. Best of luck!

10

MEASURING RECRUITMENT SUCCESS

"What gets measured, gets managed." – Peter Drucker

Key Recruitment Metrics

If you've ever wondered how to measure the effectiveness of your recruitment process, welcome to the club. It's a question that keeps many business owners up at night, especially those in the manufacturing and engineering industry. You're not alone.

The truth is, gauging the success of your recruitment strategy isn't as mystical or elusive as it might seem. Just like in your welding or CNC operations, there are metrics you can track to give you a clear picture of how well you're doing. Let's break it down.

Time to Hire

Imagine you run a CNC machine shop. One of your skilled operators takes a new job elsewhere. How long will it take you to replace him? This is where your time to hire metric comes in.

In this context, time to hire refers to the period from when you post a job vacancy to when the new employee starts. It's a measure of how quickly you can attract and onboard new talent.

If your time to hire is short, congratulations! It means you're efficient at finding and onboarding new staff. But if it's taking you months to fill a position, you might need to re-evaluate your recruitment process.

In the fast-paced world of manufacturing and engineering, time is money. A long time to hire means you're spending more resources on recruitment and potentially losing out on productivity. So, keep a close eye on this metric. It could be the difference between meeting your targets and falling behind the competition.

Quality of Hire

Now, let's move onto the quality of hire. In the engineering world, we understand quality. It's the difference between a perfectly welded joint and one that fails under pressure. The same principle applies to hiring.

The quality of hire is about how well a new employee performs in their role. It's measured by their productivity, their contribution to the team, and their overall fit within the company culture.

Here's the kicker: a high-quality hire will not only perform well but also stick around, reducing your turnover rate (more on that later). They bring value to your company, driving productivity and inspiring their colleagues.

But how do you measure this? Start with setting clear performance indicators for each role. This could be the number of CNC parts produced per hour, the precision of a welding job, or the level of customer satisfaction. Then, track how well your new hires meet these indicators.

Remember, quality beats quantity any day. It's better to invest time and resources in finding a high-quality hire than to rush and end up with a poor fit.

Cost per Hire

The last metric on our list is the cost per hire. This is the total amount you spend to attract, recruit, and onboard a new employee. It takes into account advertising costs, recruitment agency fees, time spent interviewing, and any other expenses related to the hiring process.

Here's why it's important: If you're spending a fortune to recruit new staff, your bottom line is going to feel it. It's essential to find a balance between investing in quality talent and managing your recruitment costs.

Consider this: Are you spending a lot on job ads but not getting quality applicants? Perhaps it's time to rethink your strategy. Maybe you could invest in a more targeted approach, like industry-specific job boards or networking events.

Or, are you spending hours interviewing candidates who aren't a good fit? It might be time to refine your job descriptions or screening process.

By keeping track of your cost per hire, you can identify areas where you could be more efficient, saving time and money.

In conclusion, recruitment is more than just filling vacancies. It's about finding the right people, at the right time, for the right cost. By focusing on these key recruitment metrics – time to hire, quality of hire, and cost per hire – you can turn your recruitment process from a guessing game into a science, leading your business to greater success.

Employee Retention Metrics

Let's dive straight into the meat of it. You've got your employees on board and they're doing great work. But how do you know they're happy and productive? And how do you make sure they stick around? The answer lies in understanding and tracking your employee retention metrics.

Employee Turnover Rate

First up is the employee turnover rate. This is a big one. It's the rate at which your employees leave your company. If you've got a high turnover rate, it means you're losing employees faster than you can hire them. And that's not a good sign.

To calculate the employee turnover rate, take the number of employees who left during a specific period and divide it by the average number of employees during that period. Then multiply by100. This will give you the percentage of employees who left during that time.

Keep in mind, industries like manufacturing and engineering tend to have higher turnover rates. It's the nature of the business. But if your rate is significantly higher than the industry average, it's time to take a closer look at what's going wrong.

Employee Satisfaction

Next up, we have employee satisfaction. This is a measure of how happy your employees are with their jobs. It's important because satisfied employees are more likely to stay with your company long term.

One way to measure employee satisfaction is through regular surveys. Ask your employees how they feel about their work, their colleagues, their compensation, and their opportunities for advancement. Remember to keep these anonymous to encourage honest feedback.

Another way to measure employee satisfaction is through one-on-one meetings. Regular check-ins with your employees can give you a more in-depth understanding of their satisfaction levels. You can ask them about any challenges they're facing, their goals for the future, and how they feel about the work they're doing.

Employee Productivity

Lastly, we have employee productivity. This is a measure of how much work your employees are getting done. High productivity means your employees are working efficiently and effectively.

To calculate employee productivity, you can divide your company's total output by the total input. The input could include hours worked, while the output could be the number of products manufactured or projects completed.

But remember, while it's important to have high productivity, it's equally important to make sure your employees aren't overworked. Overworked employees can quickly lead to burnout and high turnover rates.

Using Metrics for Continuous Improvement

Now, let's talk about the big picture. You've got your metrics, but what do you do with them?

Analysing Recruitment Data

The first step towards utilising metrics for continuous improvement is effective analysis of recruitment data. This data is a goldmine of information, offering insights into what's working and what's not in your hiring process.

Start with a thorough analysis of your key recruitment metrics. Delve into your 'time to hire', 'cost per hire', and 'quality of hire' metrics. Look for patterns and trends. Are there any bottlenecks slowing down your hiring process? Are certain roles more expensive to fill than others? Are some hires performing better than the rest? Answering these questions will help you identify areas that need improvement.

Next, turn your attention to your employee retention metrics. Examine your 'employee turnover rate', 'employee satisfaction', and 'employee productivity' metrics. Are you losing employees faster than you can hire them? Are your employees happy and productive? Identifying these trends can help you pinpoint issues in your retention strategies.

Don't forget to also consider industry benchmarks. Compare your metrics with industry standards. Are you ahead or lagging behind? This comparative analysis can provide a clear picture of where you stand in the market.

Making Data-Driven Decisions

Once you've analysed your recruitment and retention data, the next step is to use this information to make data-driven decisions. You see, data isn't just numbers on a spreadsheet. It's a roadmap to better business practices.

For instance, if your analysis reveals that certain positions are more expensive to fill, you might decide to invest more in training existing staff to fill these roles, rather than hiring externally. Or, if you find that your employees are leaving due to lack of career advancement opportunities, you might choose to implement a more transparent promotion process.

The key here is to let the data guide your decision-making process. Don't rely on gut feelings or intuition. Make decisions based on hard evidence. Remember, in the world of engineering and manufacturing, precision is king.

Monitoring Trends and Patterns

Keeping track of trends and patterns in your recruitment and retention metrics is the final piece of the puzzle. This is a continuous process, not a one-time event. Regular monitoring can help you spot emerging trends, allowing you to proactively address potential issues before they become major problems.

For example, if you notice a steady increase in your 'time to hire' metric, it could indicate a growing inefficiency in your hiring process. Similarly, a sudden spike in your 'employee turnover rate' could signal dissatisfaction among your staff. Keeping an eye on these trends will enable you to take timely action and prevent minor issues from escalating.

In addition, monitoring trends and patterns can also help you spot opportunities for growth. Perhaps you notice that your highest quality hires come from a particular source. In this case, you might decide to allocate more resources to that source to attract more high-quality candidates.

In essence, using metrics for continuous improvement is all about being proactive rather than reactive. It's about identifying opportunities and challenges before they become apparent and taking action to continuously enhance your recruitment and retention strategies.

Using data to drive improvement isn't just smart business practice; it's an essential strategy for surviving and thriving in the cut-throat world of engineering and manufacturing. So, dig into your metrics, make data-driven decisions, and keep an eye on trends and patterns. With this approach, you'll be well on your way to building a recruitment and retention strategy that not only attracts and retains top talent but also drives revenue and business growth.

RECAP AND ACTION ITEMS

Alrighty, let's wrap this up and get down to what you really want: action items. You've learned the essential recruitment metrics: time to hire, quality of hire, and cost per hire. Remember, these aren't just numbers. They're the pulse of your recruitment process. They'll tell you if your efforts are paying off or if you're just spinning your wheels.

Next, you dove into employee retention metrics. You now know the importance of keeping track of your turnover rate, employee satisfaction, and productivity. These are your indicators of whether your people are happy, motivated, and adding value to your business. Neglect these and you risk losing your irreplaceable team members.

Lastly, you got the lowdown on how to use these metrics for continuous improvement. You should be analysing your recruitment data, making data-driven decisions, and monitoring trends and patterns. This isn't a one-time thing. It's a cycle that needs to be repeated over and over again to keep your recruitment strategy sharp and effective.

Now, here's what you need to do:

1. Set up a system to regularly track and record your key recruitment and retention metrics. Whether you use a spreadsheet, a software, or an old-school notebook, the important thing is that you're consistent.

2. Review these metrics regularly. This isn't something to do just when there's a problem. Make it a habit. It's like checking your car's oil or tyre pressure. Regular maintenance prevents major breakdowns.

3. Use the data to inform your decisions. If your time to hire is too long, maybe you need to streamline your interview process. If your turnover rate is high, it might be time to improve your company culture or benefits.

4. Keep an eye on trends and patterns. If you notice a sudden spike in turnover or a drop in productivity, don't ignore it. Dig deeper, find out why, and address it.

5. Don't get complacent. Even if everything looks great now, don't rest on your laurels. Keep improving, keep refining, and keep striving for the best.

Remember, the success of your business is directly linked to the success of your recruitment and retention strategies. So, put these action items into play and let's start engineering your success!

ENGINEERING YOUR FUTURE SUCCESS, TODAY!

Finally, we have reached the end of our journey. It's been a whirlwind of insights, stories, and strategies. You've discovered the secrets of hiring in manufacturing and engineering, and learned how to attract the crème de la crème of the talent pool. You've learned how to not only ace interviews but turn them into job offers, and you've discovered the key to retaining staff in this competitive market.

Moreover, you've understood how to leverage recruitment agencies for success, and have been given the tools to revolutionise your hiring process. But this isn't the end of your journey. It's just the beginning. It's now time to put everything you've learned into action and transform your career or company.

Remember, the power to change is in your hands. The tools and strategies you've garnered from this book are your stepping stones to success. But they'll only work if you implement them. It's not enough to know what to do; you need to actually do it. The world rewards those who take action, not those who merely know what action to take.

So how will you apply what you've learned? Will you revamp

your hiring process to attract top talent? Will you leverage recruitment agencies to save time and streamline your hiring process? The choice is yours. But remember, every choice you make, every action you take, will shape your future.

If you're feeling overwhelmed, remember that you're not alone. There are professionals out there who can help you navigate the complex world of hiring and retention. If you need help implementing the strategies you've learned, don't hesitate to ask for it. Remember, asking for help isn't a sign of weakness; it's a sign of strength. It shows that you're committed to your success and that you're willing to do whatever it takes to achieve it.

So, if you feel that you need some professional assistance, I encourage you to get in touch. Email ibeason@beasonrecruitmentgroup.com and let's have a conversation about how you can transform your hiring process and ensure your company's success.

As we close this chapter of your journey, remember that this is only the beginning. The future is in your hands. You have the power to shape it, to mould it, to make it whatever you want it to be. You've been given the tools, now it's up to you to use them.

As we part ways, I want you to remember one thing: the success of your company or career isn't determined by the number of employees you have, the size of your office, or how much money you make. It's determined by the people you hire, the team you build, and the culture you cultivate.

So go forth, armed with the wisdom you've garnered from this book, and start creating a future of success. It's time to take control of your hiring process, to attract the top talent, and to build a team that will propel your company or career to new heights.

Thank you for embarking on this journey with me. I hope that the insights and strategies you've gained have given you a new perspective on hiring and retaining staff in the manufacturing and engineering industry.

Until our paths cross again, remember these words: "The only limit to our realisation of tomorrow will be our doubts of today." Don't let doubt hold you back. Take action, and start engineering your future success, today!

www.ingramcontent.com/pod-product-compliance
Lightning Source LLC
Chambersburg PA
CBHW050108230526
45470CB00004B/1733